GREAT PERSONALITIES

(West Bengal, Bihar and Odisha)

Dr. Mrs. Bratati Dasgupta Ph.D.

MAHA BODHI BOOK AGENCY
4-A, Bankim Chatterjee Street
Kolkata-700 073
2017

GREAT PERSONALITIES
BY
DR. MRS. BRATATI DASGUPTA

First Published 2017

Published by :
D.L.S. Jayawardana
MAHA BODHI BOOK AGENCY
4-A, Bankim Chatterjee Street
Kolkata-700 073
Ph : 9831077368
9831529452

DTP Composed by :
P.K. Bandyopadhyay
Konnagar, Hooghly

Printed at :
Sagarika Press
9 Antony Bagan Lane
Kolkata-700 009

₹ 250/-

ISBN : 978-93-84721-56-5

Preface

The book : 'Great Personalities' deals with those great men of Bengal, Bihar and Odisha, who had a significant roles to play in the history of India. Their lives were characterised by their immense strength of struggle and humanity, almost unparalleled in the Indian history. Sometimes they had to struggle alone, sometimes in association with others, in the midst of deceptions and failures to achieve their goals. In fact, India could break its slavery and achieve its position in the international level due to the service and devotion of these great people of India. Among them many were politicians who with their brave and noble efforts took active parts to make India free. Their ideals, strength of will and conscience presented an endeavour to redeem society from its narrowness. Some took recourse to literature to deal with the joys and sorrows of mankind or with the rise and fall of a nation with the help of their creative ability, so that a man can know his true self properly. The scientific genius of many satisfied the curiosity of man, their outstanding contributions in the field of science open up a new page in the history of science in the land. Though much remains to be done for India to keep pace with the advanced countries, much has been done by such contributions.

The book is written with the purpose of making the readers specially the youngones, appreciate the achievements of the great personalities of India. Their lifestyle, their various interests, hobbies, their enlightened thoughts and ideas (sometimes with the help of some ancedotes and their famous utterances, sometimes some comments made by some great people, other than those great personalities, already mentioned to establish the issue), are delineated in such a way that those will serve as an ideal for the readers who will definitely be benefitted and will really enjoy it for it has got some values from the moral point of view. In fact the book is an attempt of understanding the lives of the well-known figures in the background of the various social dimensions. In these days of modern technology, when the people are eager to know the unseen and the unknown with the help of Internet, the book will serve as a source of aesthetie pleasure, apart from its moralistic value.

Contents

West Bengal

Chapter I

Raja Ram Mohan Roy

In the past we were to obey certain customs of our society blindly. But unfortunately those proved really harmful for us. One of the cruel customs among the Hindus was 'Sati', practice. Do you know what it was? When a woman's husband died, that woman was burnt alive against her wishes with her husband's dead body. Only one man strongly refused to obey such practice—the person was Raja Ram Mohan Roy.

He was born in Hooghly, on 22nd May, 1772. Ram Mohan's father Ram Kanta Roy, was an orthodox Hindu, strictly following the Shastra and his mother Tarini Devi, was a woman of intelligence and discipline. After finishing his early study in the village-school, he was sent to Patna to learn Arabic and Persian languages. From Patna he was sent to Benaras to study Sanskrit. While learning Sanskrit at Benaras, a great change came over his mind by reading some books. He came to believe that God is one and couldn't put faith in the images of deities, we generally worship. He could easily win with his views in any kind of argument. Therefore once when a Pandit came to discuss with him on the subject of 'Tantras', he took time and within a day prepared himself to argue with him and defeated him finally in argument. He was so firm in his way that even his father couldn't change his view and he had to leave home finally.

The daring Rammohan started travelling different parts of India, including Tibet. In Tibet he was shocked to find that the Tibetian worshiped the Lama, a living man who bore certain distinguishing marks on his person as the Creator. His spirited protest against it nearly cost his life and after four years he was reconciled with his father.

By the age of twenty two, Rammohan had also learnt the English language and gained a correct knowledge of it. After serving at Bhagalpur and other places, he went to Rangpur as an assistant to the revenue officer Mr. John Digby in 1809. While living there, he devoted his leisure hours to serious study and discussions with the Hindus, Muslims etc. After the departure of Digby in 1814, Rammohan resigned his service at the East India Company that he held so long and settled down at Kolkata.

Years ago, while he was at Murshidabad, he wrote a book, called "Tuhfat-ul-Muwahhidin" (A gift to Monotheists), written in Persian language with his views against the idea that gods are many. He emphasised the presence of one Supreme Being who is the source of creation. It is mankind who gives different forms to one Eternal Being. So his mission of life was to remove from the minds of the Indians their blind belief in rituals, customs and superstitions and he established Brahmosabha, later known as Brahmo Samaj which inspired people to go by the basic principles of *Upanishad.*

After his settlement in Kolkata, he devoted his time to the improvement of his country in matters of religion, social and educational systems. In religion he did not reject the authority of the Shastras, but maintained that man's highest belief must be established on the basis of his commonsense and rationality rather than on the evidence of Shastras. In 1815, Rammohan founded Atmiya Sabha or association for the discussion of religious subjects though the orthodox Hindus opposed his thoughts. He translated the *Vedanta*

Sutra into Bengali in 1815 and Vedantasar in Bengali in 1816.

Rammohan's social reforms mainly revolved round a fight to improve the status of women. He fought bravely against the rite of becoming "Sati". One incident specially made him to take such a step. When his brother Jagamohan died, his wife Alokmanjari was found to adopt sati practice when her mother-in-law who was a widow, was alive. Ultimately Rammohan, with the help of Bentinck, the Governor General of his time, put a stop to it in 1829.

Rammohan made a noble appeal in defence of the rights of women. His dislike for polygamy and child marriage was so great that he looked for every possible occasion to oppose it. Since in those days. Brahmanas could marry several times Rammohan was married thrice though he was against such marriage. One of his friends, Nanda Kishore, was shown a beatiful girl whom he agreed to marry. But at the time of marriage, he had to marry a dark girl. Out of anger, Nanda Kishore wanted to marry again to take revenge upon his father-in-law. Then Rammohan went to him and requested him not to marry again.

During Rammohan's time, caste system was so rigid that some girls had to remain unmarried for the failure of their parents to obtain for them husbands of appropriate caste-status. As a social reformer Rammohan felt sorry for those who were such victims and believed that when India would be free from such distinctions of caste and creed,. it could form a nation of unity.

He had also great contribution in the field of education. It was through his constant efforts and the help of David Hare that Hindu College was opend in 1817. In 1816, he started a school with English as a subject of study at Kolkata. Rammohan's educational activities led to the establishment of Vedanta college in 1825 at the same place where one could study the Hindu and Christian scriptures with freedom.

In the early 19th century, the Bengali prose, a mixture of Sanskrit words, was introduced by the pundits. The first attempt to write a Bengali grammar for the people of Bengal was undertaken by Rammohan Roy. He wrote a "Grammar of the Bengali Language" *(Gaudiya Vyakaran)*. The first prose work of Rammohan was the *Vedanta Grantha* published in 1815. It was an original writing in Bengali prose without any Sanskrit words.

Thus Rammohan Roy brought about certain changes in the life of the Indians. He was to rise up against any wrongs done to any body, even to himself. While being employed in East India company, he had to go to some places at Bhagalpore on some business in palanquin. At that time, he could bravely disobey the order of a British officer, passing that way, when he ordered him to walk on foot, seeing him to be an Indian. He had also a kind heart for all. So he could freely mix up with the coolies of the street and tried to know about their problems. But Rammohan did not remain satisfied up to that points. On April 1831, he landed on Liverpool harbour. He visited England as a special envoy of the Mughal Emperor Akbar II, who had been deprived by the British Government of all his princely rights and he was successful in his mission. So Akbar II conferred the title 'Raja' on him.

On the other hand, he was the man first to realise that without books he could not express his thoughts and feelings to all. He can be called the father of Bengali prose for it was he who laid the foundation of it. However the strain of overwork wrought havic on Rammohan and at Staple Grove, near Bristol he fell ill and died in 1833.

Chapter II
Iswar Chandra Vidyasagar

The wall clock of the Church announced that it was late hours of the night. A boy came out of his house with books and began to read in the light of the lamp, of the street. He didn't have enough money to light a lamp in his house at night. So after sleeping for sometime, he spent the rest of the night by reading in that way. Yet he was given the title, "Vidyasagar". I think at least some of you who love "Barna Parichay', must know his name. His actual name was Ishwar Chandra Banerjee.

He was born in Birsingha village of Midnapore in 1820. From the very childhood, Ishwar Chandra was very naughty. He had the habit of eating the fruits of the neighbours stealthily or sometimes he used to make the wet clean cloth to be dried up in the sun of some neighbours, dirty, or while passing by the paddy field, often he used to destroy some ears of corn by picking those up at premature time. He had again the habit of doing the opposite of what he was told to do. His father Thakurdas Banerjee knowing his nature, always asked him to do a thing, though he really meant the opposite of it. For example, if the clothes were not washed which Iswar would wear at school, his fathers used to advise his son, "Iswar, today you should better wear a clean cloth." But Iswar without understanding the implication of what his father meant, wore dirty clothes.

After completing his education at village-school, successfully, with the help of his excellent memory, on the advice of the village head Pundit Kalikanta Chattopadhay, that Iswar should learn English, Thakurdas took Iswar to Kolkata, for further study. On the way, while he was walking on foot with his father, he learnt to memorise English numbers simply by counting the milestones as he had a great merit and memory. Even his father was quite astonished by his memory.

After coming to Kolkata, both Thakurdas and Iswar lived at Burrabazar where Iswar was admitted to the local pathshala. In spite of the advice of some, that Iswar should learn English thoroughly, after completion of his education at the local pathshala, Thakurdas, gradually got him admitted to Sanskrit College on his own decision as he himself could not learn it properly because of the lack of means, since his father was poor. Iswar had to study with much trouble. After completing all his household works, he had go to the college though he had no complain against his troubles. In the college he came out in all classes successfully after having a great deal of proficiency in Naya, Grammar, literature. He completed his education at Sanskrit College and got several awards and scholarships. In spite of all difficulties, he did excellently well in all examinations and was given the title 'Vidyasagar' as nobody before him had done so well.

After completing his education, he began to teach at Fort William College. In spite of his vast knowledge in Sanskrit and Bengali he also became an expert in English and Hindi.

Afterwards he became the editor of Sanskrit College which was during his time in the midst of crisis. Later on when he was given the post of professor, he refused it straight and instead referred the name of his friend Taranath Bachaspati, as he was in financial trouble. He himself personally as a mark of friendship went to him at Kalna to convey him the news of his appointment as no messenger was available within a short time.

But because of the difference of opinion with the chief editor Rasamoy Datta, he resigned from his post, though in his time, the chaotic condition of the college came to an end. Soon he was given a call again from Fort William College with a higher salary. But Vidyasagar was reappointed in Sanskrit College because of his ability and skill of work and later on became the principal of the college. Even, he also got appointment from Education department in the post of Inspector of Schools.

He as a Inspector of Schools, went to several places and set up many primary and high schools in villages and cities for the development of education. In Kolkata he established Metropolitan Institution which got recognition from Kolkata University to impart education on college level. He with the help of Mr. Bethune the Govenor General established Hindu Balika Vidyalaya (later on Bethune College) for women education in the country. He wrote many books though some are translations for us in various subjects such as *Barnaparichay, Betal Panchabingsati, Sakuntala. Kathamala, Bodhoday, Prabhabati Sambhasan* (unfinished) etc. in lucid and simple language. He also also introduced punctuations to make Bengali language much more easier and pleasant to read. To make Sanskrit language much more easy, he wrote "Byakaran Upakramonika" and "Byakara Kaumadi". He even introduced summer vacation in schools for children and teachers.

As a man he was kind to all. He often fed the poor freely and helped them in troubles. On the night of a winter, while passing through a street, he found a man, shivering in cold. Without hesitation, he gave away his wrapper to give him comfort. He even helped Michael Madhusudan in distress by lending money from others. On the other hand, he had great respect for his parents. While studying in Sanskrit College, he was married to Dinamayee of Shatrughara Bhattacharjee of Khirpai village at the age of fourteen on his father's wish, though he wanted to dedicate his life for the welfare of his country. On another occasion, his mother Bhagabati Devi gave him some urgent call. As he was not granted leave at first, he was ready to resign from the post. Then his leave was granted. After taking many troubles, even by swimming across the Damodar river, he reached his native village to meet his mother out of great love for her.

Like Rammohan Roy, Ishar Chandra made certain changes in society to enlighten the conservative Indians. Like Rammohan's horrible custom of "Sati" he took initiative to introduce widow re-marriages as he felt much for the Hindu widows who had to lead a very strict life. He even went further to bear the expenses of such marriage on his own. But as he had no adequate amount of money, he asked help from the rich, even some kindhearted Britishers also helped him in this regard. In deed many such marriges took place under his charge. But to bear the expenses of widow re-marrige he had also to borrow money from the money-lenders. Even he approved of his own son's marriage with a widow. Again he tried to put an end to a custom in which a Brahmin could marry several times. The laws to abolish social injustices like widow re-marriage passed in his favour in due course of time in 1856.

He also took a great step to spread women education with the assistance of Mr. Bethune as women in his time had to bear a very disgraceful life though he had to tolerate resistance in everykind of his social acts.

Ishwar Chandra Vidyasagar, throughout his life fought against the wrongs of the society of his time. He was a true leader who felt the need to educate every class of people of our country. Such a great man died in 1891. He will forever be remembered for his vast knowledge, kindness, sacrifice and dedication.

Chapter III
Rabindranath Tagore

Now I will tell you about a boy of a wealthy family whose childhood days were mostly spent under the care of the servants of the house. They often made him sit by the window-side. Then they used to draw a boundary line with a warning to him that if he would cross the line, something bad would take place. The boy spent his time by looking through the window at the sky, trees and the people, walking on the street. The name of that boy was Rabindranath Tagore. Rabindranath Tagore sings for us the songs of all the time. He got world fame as a poet, dramatist, novelist and thinker. He also acted well, sang a great many songs and did very good pictures.

He was born at Jorasanko in Kolkata on May 7, 1861 in a wealthy family. He was the youngest son of Debendranath Tagore and the grandson of Prince Dwaraka Nath Tagore. Rabindranath at first studied at home. Then one day he saw his elder brother going to school. Then he began to cry for he wanted to go to school. At that time his teacher who taught him at home told him—"Well you are now crying for not sending you to school. A time will come when you will more cry for sending you to school." That became quite true in his later life. However he was atfirst admitted to Oriental Seminary and then to Normal School. But he had to study much outside his school subjects. When he was eight years old, his nephew Jyotiprasad one day gave him a blue excise book and told him to write poems. From then on, he started writing poems on his own. Again when he was reading at Normal School, one of his teachers, seeing his interest in writing poems, wrote two lines in form of a poem and asked him to write the next two lines. Rabindranath could easily compose the other two which matched really well. The teacher then encouraged him and said, "Well, you will be a poet one day."

Once Rabindranath was unwilling to go to school since his head had been shaven in order to get him ready for the sacred thread ceremoney. His anxiety however was however relieved when his father Debendranath decided to take his son to the Himalayas. It was in course of this journey, that Rabindranath first resided at Shantiniketan. Debedranath had enjoyed the beauty of the peaceful spot during a previous trip and simply bought it. However after their return from the Himalayas, he did not like to go to school for it looked like a prison to Rabi. After the death of his mother Saradasundri whom he lost at the age of fourteen (though he didn't get much care from his mother), it was impossible for anyone to send him to school. In this way he left the school and started studying under the care of the home tutor though after a time, he read at an English school for some time.

As Rabindranath could not only compose poems but also could sing, his father one day on the eve of Maghatshab, called him up and told him to sing one of the new songs written by himself, accompanied by the harmonium played by Jyotiprakash. Rabindranath gladly sang before him. Debendranath hearing his song was so happy that he gave him the reward of five thousands rupees, a reward won by Rabi for the first time.

At the age of seventeen, his second brother Satyndranath took him to England for higher study. After a time, he came back to Kolkata because of his dislike for English system of education. Further he began to take interest in writing poems like "Nirjharer Swapna Bhonga" and "Sandya Sangeet" and the musical drama like "Balmiki Pratibha". At that time, he went one day to attend a marriage ceremony at the house of Ramesh Chandra Dutta, the great historian, There Bamkim Chandra Chatterjee, the great Bengali novelist was highly honoured with a garland. But Bankim Chandra praised Rabindranath for his writing "Sandhya Sangeet" and said, "This garland which I wear is best suited for Rabindranath."

Rabindranath went on writing after 'Balmiki Pratibha' "Kalmrigaya"—another lyrical drama. He even went to the extent of enacting his own musical drama like "Balmiky Pratibha" on the stage where he himself played the role and won a great deal of praise.

After his visit to Karoar, a hilly place of Karnat, where his poetic skill became much settled at a very young age, he was given in marriage with Bhobatarini the daughter of the Supervisor of his estate, Benimadhav. After the marriage his wife was named Mrinalini.

Next Rabindranath spent sometime at Shilaidaha to supervise his father's business affairs. He was charmed by the poetic beauty of the place which served as a background for some of his poems and short stories. In 1911, Bangiya Sahitya Parishad felicitated the poet by presenting him a golden lotus.

In spite of his fame, he also had to face some miserable incidents like the death of Mirinalini Devi in 1902 also the death of his daughter Renuka and in 1905 the death of his youngest son Samindra. But he did not feel dejected and became world famous as a poet.

Besides he wanted to rouse patriotic feeling among the Indians and wrote some patriotic songs for the Independence of India. His "Janaganamona" is our national song. He gave away his knighthood after the brutal incident at Jallianwalabagh at Punjab. Even Gandhiji was charmed by his poetric personality.

Since Tagore was famous as a worldspoet we should know about his important poetic works like *Manashi, Sonar Tori, Kalpana, Naibedya, Kheya* etc. His best known works are *Chokher Bali, Naukadubi, Gora, Ghore Baira, Shesher Kabita* etc and his greatest dramas are *'Visarjan', 'Chandalika', 'Raja', 'Dakghar', 'Raktakarabi'* etc. His short stories like *'Kabuliwallah', 'Khokababur Pratyabartan'*, 'Subha', 'Chhuti', 'Atithi', should be remembered by all.

His most important poetical work is *'Gitanjali'*. He went abroad with his Gitanjali and its translation received wide publicity. The poet yeats took the charge of printing 'Gitanjali'. In 1913, Tagore was awarded Nobel prize (named after Alfred Nobel, the engineer and scientist of Sweden) by the Swedish Academy. Apart from it, he also received wide applause everywhere outside India for his poetic talent. Sometime, before his death, he was awarded D.Lit degree from Oxford University.

But his greatest achievement was to establish an open air school at Santiniketan. In that school, the teaching was given in open space under the trees. Later on it developed into university called Vishwa Bharati. Near Bolpur was set up, Sriniketan, where training on agriculture, leather work etc. is given.

At last Tagore's long life came to an end. He passed away on August 7, 1941. It was a great loss for the whole world.

Chapter IV
Kazi Najrul Islam

A young boy used to work in a bakery shop at the salary of Rs five except food and lodging. But when he used to take his food in the shop every day, a beggar would come and stand near the shop. The boy had the habit of giving him from his share daily as he well knew what hunger was. Then oneday he found him lying dead on the street. Such a sight gave him much pain. He, himself, staying without food through out the day did the last rites of the beggar with the help of some money. The young boy was Kazi Nazrul Islam, the revolutionary poet of our country.

His birth (1899) took place in the village of Churulia of Burdwan. His father name was Kazi Fakir Ahamed and his mother was Zaheda Khatun. Though Fakir Ahamed was very pious in heart, his financial condition was not good. As his birth took place in the midst of misery, Nazrul was named 'Dhukhu Mia'.

Nazrul from his very childhood was beloved to everybody. He started learning songs from his brother Kazi Sahebjan and by his sweet voice he started attracted every body. Nazrul started his education at the age of four or five. But his father died at his age of eight. Then he started learning Arabian and Persian languages from his uncle who got him admitted to a school in their village Churulia. At the sametime, he could compose very beautiful poems in Persian language which he learned so well.

But as his father died, when he was quite young, Nazrul had to earn money some way or others. He started earning money by reading and explaining the *Koran* at various places. He also developed a great zeal for reading various religious books like the *Ramayana*, the *Mahabbharata*, the *Puranas* in Bengali language. However in the midst of trouble, he passed lower primary examination at the age of ten. He got the job of teaching 'Dharapat' in the school even at that age and also used to call the Muslims for the prayer meeting in the Mosque in the morning and in the evening. However because of his misery and wants, his education remained incomplete. So he left his village and took his job in a bakery shop. But as he had inborn quality for singing songs, which he inherited from his elder brother and his uncle, he always attended the function on musical performance. At the same time he went on composing poems also. At that time he joined a group called 'Leto which was famous for a kind of musical tournament and went on singing with them at various places. Also he wrote musical plays, narrating the stories of the Hindu mythology and the folk tales. But this activity also didn't last long for him. With the help of a distant relative he was admitted to Siarshol High School. Because of his responsibility of maintaining his family, he left his education again incomplete. After sometime however he was admitted, to Marthun school (with the help of another relative) in class VI at the age of twelve, where the headmaster was Kumud Ranjan Mullick whom Najrul liked very much. But after a short period, he again had to take a job at a bakery. But by the favour of the police officer Raffijuddin Saheb, Nazural again was admitted to a high school at Dabirampur at Mymansingha. There he was admitted to class VII. In spite of his disruption of studies for the time being, he again got admission at Siarshol high school in class VIII. There he got stipend of rupees five for being a brilliant student and after getting double promotion was promoted to class X. At the same time, he went on reading Bengali and English literature and the poems of Rabindranath. In 1916, his poem 'Mukti' was published in a magazine "Bangia Muslim Sahitya".

During the time of The First World War, Nazrul and his friend Sailajananda Mukherjee planned to join the army force and to learn the use of weapons, to fight war against the British Government. Sailajananda was not successful to join the army but Nazrul passed the medical test to do the training at Karachi army quarters. At Karachi, he was promoted to the post of Habildar. But after a time he came back to Kolkata. Nazrul met Mazaffar Ahamad, a well known personalality and the meeting brought a new change in his life. With his help, Nazrul started "Dainik Nabayug", a magazine and became the chief editor of "Dhumketu" magazine.

But the British Government arrested Nazrul who was kept in Presidency Jail for expressing revolutionary ideas through such magazine. Next he was kept in Alipur Central Jail and later on he was sent to Hooghly and Baharampur jail. In 1923 he was released from the prison.

After sometime, while staying at Krishnagore with his wife Pramiladevi, Nazrul's son Arindam Khalid was born. But he was called Bulbul by all. When after a time, Bulbul died of pox, it was a great shock for Nazrul. To Nazrul the shock was so great that once when some police and an officer came for a search in his house, he was unwilling to make them search a tin box. When they forced him to open the box, it was found that the box had nothing but some toys and dresses of Bulbul. Such was Nazrul's love for his son. At the same time he went on writing to inspire the people of his country. Even while in prison at Baharampur, he staged his own play with the prisoners. The youths again became excited by Nazrul's article "Dharmaghot" published in "Nabayug" magazine. Even his poem "Bidrohi", published in "Bijoli" magazine was greatly praised by Tagore. Nazrul's important works an *Agnibina, Phanimansa, Dolonchampa, Chhayanot* etc. which are well to remember.

Nazrul was a great lover of children and for them he wrote many poems which are attractive to be read.

In due course, Nazrul did service for sometime at a Grammaphone Company. Suddently after a time, he became senseless and dumb. He was even sent to foreign countries for treatment. But it was too late. At last Nazrul Islam breathed his last at Dacca in 1975. Kazi Nazrul Islam throughout his life, was inspired by the spirit of protest against the British tyranny and his poetry will forever create a lasting effect on our minds.

Chapter V

Bankim Chandra Chatterjee

It was early morning in the city of Kolkata. A gentleman was reading a book in his drawing room. At that time, a messenger came to him with a letter from his friend. The gentleman returned the letter of his friend immediately. He also wrote a letter to his friend, "I am a Bengalee : You are also a Bengalee. Why do you write in English ? Have you forgotten Bengali ?"—a letter which reveals his great love for the Bengali language. The name of the gentleman was Bankim Chandra Chatterjee.

Bankim Chandra was born in the village Kathalpara of 24 Parganas in 1838. His father's name was Jadavchandra Chatterjee and his mother's name was Durga Sundari who was an ideal lady. At his age of five, a ceremony was arranged on the eve of his first lesson in writing. The priest of the family wrote on the floor two vowels. Then he erased the two letters. But little Bankim could easily write those without seeing those two letters of the alphabet. His maternal grandfather frankly told that his grand son would later on become a great man. It proved true that the child Bankim could easily learn letters of the alphabet from his home—tutor within a day. Atfirst Bankim chandra was admitted to a high school of English medium of Midnapur where he showed great merit specially in English. He couldn't read in one school at a stretch, since his father had to go to different places, being a government employee. So next he was admitted to Hooghly College. There also he soon became known as a meritorious student.

After his marriage with Mohini Devi, even at the age of twelve he started writing poems. Actually at Kathalpara, he could easily recite Sanskrit poems because of his close association with pandit named Haladhar Tarkachuramoni. While reading in Hooghly College, he could earn a great deal of proficiency in grammar, literature and poetry in the school of Sriram Nayabagish. In 1952, he got an award of twenty rupees for his poem "Kaminiukti" in a poetry competition organised by "Sambad Probhakar" a magazine which became famous in those days.

While he was in third year of Hooghly College he left Hooghly College. According to the wish of his father, he got admission to Presidency College of Kolkata to read law. In 1857, when Kolkata University was established, he passed in the first division in the Entrance Examination. Even in 1858 when graduation examination was introduced in Kolkata University, he also stood first in the examination. According to the wish of his father, he became Deputy Magistrate at the age of twenty at Jessore. When he was at Khulna on service his first wife Mohini Devi died and at his parents request he was married to Rajlakshi who belonged to the famous Choudhury family of Halisahar. Later on she became the source of his inspiration.

When he was transferred from Khulna to Negua near Kathi of Midnapur, he one day saw a saint, worshipping Goddess Kali and a woman in white dress in the dead of night. He was very much charmed by such a beautiful sight and wrote his *Kapal Kundala* there. At that time, he played a vital role in removing the torture of the British upon indigo planters and himself resisted theft and robbery.

According to the order of the British, some skilled fighters with sticks were sent to deal with the farmers who refused to plant indigo in stead of paddy. The fighters with sticks looted the farmers and set fire to their houses. The ruler of the subdivision of the district handled the situation effectively. The guilty were put to trial as a result of judgement—one was hanged and the thirty four were given lifeterm imprisonment. The administrator was Bankim Chandra. But in the midst of such troubles, he wrote his first novel *Durgeshnandini.*

From Alipur as a Deputy Collector, he came to Beharampur at Murshidabad. At that time, he was recognised as a great novelist of Bengali literature; soon he became the editor of 'Banga Darshan' and his novels and articles began to be published one by one in the magazine 'Banga Darshan'. In 1882, while he was the deputy Magistrate at Alipore, his *Ananda Math* was published which served as a source of inspiration to the freedom fighters of India.

Bankim Chandra had the courage to make a strong protest against the injustices done by the British in his time. One incident of his life best reveals his nature. Oneday in his early years, he found when he was walking in the street that a few English soldiers had made some dogs to attack his younger brother. He also saw that his brother was very afraid of facing those dogs. He scolded those soldiers—"Are you showing bravery in that way ? Stop your dogs from doing so."

The soldiers felt a great shame and soon did as they were asked to do. At that time it was not easy to warn the English soldiers in that way.

On the other hand, he didn't even hesitate to admire a man of true merit like Madhusudan Datta and Rabindranath Tagore.

Bankim Chandra had his own independent way of thinking. Therefore he could write such great novels like *Durgeshnandini, Mrinalini, Rajsinha, Kapalkundala, Bishbrikha, Rajani, Krishna Kanter Will, Anadamath, Debichaudhuirani* etc. His last work was *Sitaram.*

Bankim Chandra, taking the help of imagination wrote the history of the Bengalees in a new way, so as to make them feel deeply the tyrany of the British upon our country. His "Bandemataram" was written with that aim in mind. This great novelist of Bengali literature died in 1894. But he lives forever in our memory for his great contribution to Bengali literature.

Chapter VI

Sarat Chandra Chatterjee

In the village school of the pandit, the most naughty boy was Sarat whose nick name was Nyara. One day the pandit went outside the school on some business, after filling up his hookah with tobacco. Sarat in the meantime, filled the hookah of the pandit with the pieces of bricks instead of tobacco. When the pandit came back, he could not smoke from his hookah. He found that in place of tobacco somebody had put some pieces of bricks in it. The pandit became angry and cried out, "Who had done it?" One of the boys told him the name of Sarat. The moment the pandit heard this, he rushed towards Sarat to beat him with a cane. But he could not catch him for he at that time ran away as fast as he could. But at the time of leaving the place, he didn't forget to give a push to the boy who had told the pandit his name. Such naughty boy was Sarat Chandra Chatterjee, the great Bengali writer of our country.

Sarat Chandra was born in a poor family in the village Debanandapur in the district of Hooghly, in the month of 15th Septermber, 1876. His father's name was Matilal Chatterjee and his mother's name was Bhubanmohini Devi. From his childhood, he was naughty indeed. Nobody could match him in stealing fruits from the trees of the neighbours, in stealing fishes at the dead of night, to catch butterflies and grasshoppers. Courage never failed him in anything. Though he was naughty he was also an expert in nursing the patients. If necessary he alone with a lantern and stick in hand had to travel distant places to call in the doctor and to bring medicines for the patients. So he was dear to his village people. Often without the knowledge of the fishermen, he used to go to the institution of Vaishnavas (where they assemble for religious worship) on their boat accompanied by his friends or some time, on foot to witness play-acting or music. In his teen age, he also joined open air opera of the dramatic party and used to travel many places with them.

He was admitted by his father when he was five, in a village school of Pari Pandit at Debanandapur and later on to a Bengali school. At that time as his father got his service in Dihiri of Bihar, Sarat Chandra had to leave the school of Debanandpur and passed his Middle School Examination (Chhatra Britti Exam.) from a school at Bhagalpur as he didn't accompany his father. Later on after passing Chhatra Britti Exam he got his admission in the district school of Bhagalpur in class IV. There he proved himself a very good student and he was given double promotion. But after a time his father again lost his job. So coming back to Debanandapur with his family, he was admitted to class VII in Hooghly Branch School. But when he was in class X he couldn't continue his study for want of money. At that time he at the age of seventeen, wrote *Kashinath*, a story about his class mate Kashinath. Then due to poverty his father again took him as well as his family to Sarat Chandra's maternal uncle's house at Bhalgalpur. There he with the help of a neigbour was admitted to Jubili Collegiate School from where he passed his Entrance Examination. But again want and poverty stood in his way but due to the favour of one of his relatives he was admitted to Jubili College but couldn't continue his study as he couldn't pay his fees of the final examination. After the death of his mother, his father, started staying in a separate house at Bhagalpur.

During that time Sarat Chandra passed his time in acting and in playing games. He also used to help the needy along with his friend Rajen Majumder, a courageous noble youth. Sarat Chandra's 'Indranath' of *Sricanta* was based on such a character. He at that time, used to visit the house of a neighbour and spent his time there in writing many stories and novels like *Bardidi, Debdas, Chandranath, Subhada* etc.

Then for a time, he left his house and roamed from place to place. While roaming, he received the death news of his father. So he had to return to Bhagalpur to perform the last rites of his father. After that, he again went to Kolkata to seek his fortune. There he got a job of translation temporarily. Before going to Burma to seek his job in 1903, he was awarded *Kuntalin* award for wrting a short story *Mandir.*

While staying at Rangoon, he got a job, with the help of one of friends. At that time he used to spend his time by closely associating himself with the workers who lived in the suburbs. He also married a girl of one of the labourers. But after the death of his wife Santi and their son (who died due to plague in Rangoon), he had to marry again Mokhhada (renamed Hiranmoyee by Sarat Chandra) in the same locality.

While staying at Rangoon, he was on leave for one month and came back to his own country. At that time his novel *'Ramer Sumati'* was published in *Jamuna* magazine. His another novel *'Bardidi'* was also published in *Bharati* magazine. But on account of his illness, he had to leave his job at Rangoon and had to come back to Kolkata and stayed at Howrah. At that time, he became quite famous as a writer by writing many novels. He was awarded the degree of D.Lit by Dacca University and also he received Jagattarini Medal from Kolkata University.

He made a great contribution in our Bengali literature. His important works are *Ramer Sumati, Bindur Chele, Mejdidi, Bardidi, Birajbou, Srikanta, Panditmahasai, Pallisamaj, Datta, Debdas, Bamanur Meye* etc. He wrote mainly about some social problems of our village of Bengal with a great deal of sympathy and pity, specially when women were the victims of such problems. He on the other hand, had a great feeling for the mother land as we find in his *'Pather Dabi'.* He had a way of writing which easily moves us. Such a man died in the 16th of January 1938. Of all the great writers, he is one in whom we most easily find a friend and therefore, we should always remember him with great respect.

Chapter VII

Sri Ramkrishna Paramahansa Deb

A man was sitting on the bank of the Ganges. He held on one hand a lump of clay and on the other a rupee. He was saying within himself, "A rupee is a lump of clay and a lump of clay is a rupee." At one time, he threw away the two in the Ganges. The man was Sri Ramkrishna Paramahansa Deb. He didn't at all like wealth, so to him the rupee and the lump of clay had the same value. To think about God was the only aim of his life. He was a great worshipper of Goddess Kali.

He was born at Kamarpukur of Hooghly district in 17th February, 1833. His father was Khudiram Chatterjee and his mother was Chadramoni Devi. He was called Gadadhar by his family members in the house, though he was later known as Sri Ramkrishna Paramhansadeb. Gadadhar at the age of five was sent to school but he had no interest for reading. He only loved to read Bengali. Being the son of a Brahmin, he loved to recite the words (used) in the prayer of the deities. After a time, he could read the *Ramayana* very beautifully in his musical tone, so everybody liked to listen to his reading. He often spent his time in making the images of gods and goddesses and in worshiping them with flowers. He also liked to mix with the saints, coming from different places.

After the death of his father, Ramkumar, Gadadhar's elder brother went to Kolkata and took his brother Gadadhar along with him. He took him to Jhamapukur where he had opened Sanskrit Grammar school. But Gaddadhar had no intention of going to school as he had no interest in bookish knowledge. Rather he took interest in learning sacred mantras and passed his time in helping his brother in worshiping. In this way, Gaddadhar became the regular priest of one of his neighbour's house. Therefore his sincere way of worshiping overwhelmed everybody and they used to give him food offered to the deity, though Gadadhar sometimes used to give away those to the beggars in the street. In fact such indifferent nature of Gadadhar made his elder brother, a little more anxious.

In the meantime, Rani Rashmoni of Janbazar established the temples of Radha Govinda, Kali, Shiva near Dakhineswar on the bank of the Ganges. Ramkumar was made the priest of Kali temple. Mathuramohan, the son-in-law of Rani Rashmoni used to look after the activities of the temple. Being impressed by the image of Shiva, created by Gadadhar, he showed it to Rani, who equally impressed by the image, appointed Gadadhar to take care of the dress of the image of Kali. A priest named Khetranath was given the charge to worship the image of Radha Gobinda. Once during the time of a festival, due to carelessness of Khetranath the priest of Radha Govinda's temple, the image dropped from his hand and one of its legs was broken. Pandits gave order to throw away the broken image and to worship a new one. Godadhar's suggestion was not to obey the order of the priest but to worship it (as he himself repaired it with clay) as there was no harm in it—such was his self confidence in doing any kind of work. Later on when Khetranath left his job, Gadadhar was appointed as the priest of Radha Gobinda temple.

After Gadadhar's initiation by Kenaram Bhattacherjee, a Brahmin, he started learning the procedure of worshiping Kali from his elder brother Ram Kumar. After sometime, while giving the charge of worshiping Kali by Gadhadhar, and his nephew Hriday, at Radha Govinda temple, Ram Kumar started for his native home to spend sometime there. But on the way, he fell sick, took shelter in a relative's house and died there. Gadadhar was really shocked hearing such news.

Mean while, returning from his native land, Gadadhar took great care in worshiping the image of Kali. But he didn't like to worship Kali like an ordinary priest. In the forest of 'Panchabati' he went on meditating on the Goddess Kali. At the end of the night, he entered the temple and instead of the image, was bent on visualising the Goddess Kali Herself. Without getting response from the still image, he got ready to kill himself with the dagger. Being moved by a strange fancy he lost his consciousness. He remained in that state more or less even the next day. Mathurbabu and Rani Rashmoni took care of him and nursed him. Again once, during the time of worship in stead of offering flowers and the leaves of wood apple to the goddess Kali, he offered those on his own head by mistake. Next moment he felt as if the image Herself was accepting his offering. When Rani Rashmoni and Mathura Mohan got information about Gadadhar's strange attitude, they both visited Dkhisneswar to know about the real affair. Rani visited the temple and sat to listen to the songs of Kali by Gadadhar. Suddenly Gadadhar gave her a slap and scolded her, "My God! you are thinking about your wealth even how ?" Everybody started rebuking him. But Gadadhar's reply was : "What am I do ? I am only obeying my Mother Kali's order." But Rani Rashmoni admitted her own fault that she really thought about a case at High Court. Sitting in the temple, Godadhar in her opinion had really done right; in fact Goddess Kali had really commended her through Gadadhar not to do so.

After six years, Gadadhar came back to Kamarpukur. There he married Saradamoni, the daughter of Ram Chandra Mukherjee of Joyrambati. After two years, he again took the charge of Kali temple at Dakhineswar. On the other hand,

Rani Rashmoni fell sick suddenly, and died at Kalighat. Gadadhar of Dakhineswar was quite moved by her death.

Once in the morning, came a female ascetic to Dakhineswar to have a look at Gadadhar. In fact she was an expert in sacred texts of Tantras, the Gita etc. Later on it was disclosed that she had come to reveal the true nature of Gadadhar and gave him the initiation of "Shakti" according to Tantras. Next also came many saints to discuss with him the essence of Sastras and they were pleased to regard him as 'Paramahansha'. After some time came Totapuri, who made him know the main significance of Vedanta. He was initiated by Totapuri who gave him the new name 'Ramkrishna Paramahansha', which means a person who like a duck could separate the milk and water and could accept only milk.

After the departure of Totapuri, came Gobinda Roy, proficient in Arabic and Persian language, who invited Ramakrishna into meditation according to Muslim religion. In this way, he engaged himself in deep meditation to know about the cult of other religions. Gradually his fame spread far and wide. Many people came to have a sight of him. Dakhineswar became a holy place for all. Ramkrishna preached before them that God is one and unique though there may be different ways to attain him. Influenced by Sri Ramkrishna many tried to follow his path. His wife Saradamoni was also a great follower of his path. Ramkrishna himself visited the house of Maharshi Debendranath, the founder of Brahmasamaj who appreciated his way of life by saying, "Well, you are really an expert player for you know well how to direct two swords at a time, the sword for work and the sword for knowledge." Even Ramkrishna had a such a noble soul that he had full appriciation for the vast learning of Vidyasagar, for he said, "So far I have seen only ponds and canals, now I have come across the vast sea." Narendranath himself came to meet Sri Ramkrishna. Though he was an educated youth, he also by his influence followed his path. Ramkrishna made him feel the touch of God, simply by touching him. In fact Ramkrishna was not only the preacher of his own ideal but he also knew how to love all from the core of his heart by purifying their souls.

At last Ramkrishna's end came in a sad way. He was affected with a fatal disease called throat cancer. He was brought to Cossipore having an open air environment. Though the doctor forbade all not to get in touch with him, but Ramkishna was far from listening to the doctor's advice and performed 'Kalpataru' festival to mix with the people of all types to give love and joy to all. At last he died in 1886. He was a great soul who not only showed love and tenderness for all but also taught all to love one another.

Chapter VIII
Vivekananda

A little boy named Bile liked to play with his friends a peculiar type of game *i.e.* to think deeply about something by closing one's eyes for long. The winner would be the one who could keep his eyes closed longer than others. One day they were playing the game. Suddenly a snake came in sight. Other boys opening their eyes noticed the snake. They cried out, "Bile Bile, a snake !" and ran away. But even that warning didn't make the little boy Bile wake from his thought. But the snake without doing any harm to him slowly passed away. Then everybody present had a sigh of relief. The little boy who had so much concentration later on became known as Swami Vivekananda.

He was born in the locality of Simla of North Kolkata in the 12th January in 1863. His father Biswanath Dutta was a famous laywer and his mother's name was Bhubaneswari Devi. After the birth of Bile, his mother gave him the name Bireswar (in short Bile) as she believed to have him by the favour of God Shiva. Bile at the time of admission was named Narendranath Dutta. He as a child had a great merit but at this same time he was very naughty. Sometimes his mother to control him used to pour cold water upon his head, all the time uttering the name of Lord Shiva and in that way he became calm and quiet.

From his childhood, he loved to listen to the stories of religious books like the *Ramayana* and the *Mahabhharata*.

He also had a great fondness for monks. One day when a monk came to their house asking for something, Bile gave away whatever he had without any thought, so he was often locked in a room whenever a monk visited his house. Still then he was found throwing away clothes through the window to the monk, standing at the bottom of it.

From the young age, Naren looked upon all the classes of people in the same way and had no distinction at all. In his father's office, there was a system that each visitor of each caste should have separate tobaco pipe to smoke. One day Naren smoke from all tobaco pipes. When his father scolded him for that, he said firmly that he saw no difference in doing that. In this way though he had enough respect for his parents, he had no fear of mind to speak out anything which he thought to be just or true.

He was also a student of great merit. He completed the syllabus of two years in one year in Entrance Examination and passed in the first division. Even in the college he was the best student. His favourite subject was Philosophy. He also had an excellent memory. He had another qualitty—he loved to sing songs. Besides he had a great curiosity to know about religion—rather the main essence of religion. He used to attend many religious gatherings to listen to the lectures of various personalities. He used to ask the speakers, "Well have you seen God ? " But nobody could give him the right answer.

Once he got an opportunity to meet Sri Ramakrishna, when he came to his locality Simla on the request of one of his disciples. Sri Ramakrishna was so much impressed by his song that he told him to visit him at Dakhineswar. When Naren went to Dakhineswar, he asked only one question to Sri Ramakrishna, "Well Sir, have you seen God ?" Ramakrishna replied, "Yes ! I have seen God. I can make you see Him also." From then on, Naren met Ramakrishna several times for he believed that Sri Ramakrishna was the only man who showed him the path to attain the blessings of God. Soon he became Sri Ramakrishna's most beloved disciple and was named Swami Vivekananda. Sri Ramakrishna advised him not to search for his own salvation but to look for salvation of all. Vivekananda followed his advice throughout his life. It was for this reason when he was in want of money after his father's death, he couldn't ask from Goddess Kali money to meet his needs but only asked for knowledge, piety, strength and confidence. It was possible for him to do so, as he was a monk by nature.

As a monk he travelled many places on feet and was sad to see the sufferings of the Indians. He wanted to remove those sufferings and the distinction between castes and creed. He wanted to preach the path of virtue and truth.

In 1893 A.D., in the city of Chicago of America, the Parliament of Religion was held. But no Indian representative was invited there. Vivekananda could easily realise that the people of the world had no idea of the Indian religion. So he decided to attend the conference without any invitation. In this respect, he got some financial help from some kings of India. When he reached Chicago, he was in great trouble. He couldn't get any room in any hotel having black complexion. At last by the favour of an American lady, he found a shelter there and also to get entrance in the conference.

In the conference, different people of different religions spoke about the greatness of their own religions. But Vivekananda had no right to speak as he as Indian representative was not invited there. At last, again by the favour of that American lady, he was permitted to speak on Hindu religion for five minutes. But when he addressed the American audience as "Sisters and Brothers of America", he earned a great deal of praise for those present were amazed as nobody before had addressed them in such an intimate tone. Even when the scheduled time was over, by the request of the audience he was given more time to speak on. Not only that day, but as long as the Parliament of Religion continued, he was permitted to speak each day on the significance of Hindu religion. So not only in America but also in many counties throughout the world, he was recognised as the great pioneer of Hindu religion and had got many disciples. When he went to England, many gathered to listen to his lectures. The rich English lady Miss Margaret Nobel became his disciple who later on known as Bhagini Nivedita (the name given by Vivekananda himself) when she came to India. Even in England he had a discussion on the life and preaching of Sri Ramakrishna with German thinker and Professor Maxmuller.

In the University of Harvard, the professors, after listening to his lectures on the Philosophy of Vedanta wanted to confer on him the post of "Chair of Eastern Philosophy" but he refused such post, claiming himself to be a saint who had come for a fruitful work and not to earn respect. Coming back to India, he set up "Ramakrishna Mission" and "Belur Math" to serve people in distress and to spread education. His foreign disciple Margaret Nobel devoted her life for the spread of education and for social service in Kolkata. To lead a lonely life for sometime, he went to the Himalayas. But when there was an attack of plague in Kolkata, many people became the victims of such disease. So he had to return to Kolkata to serve the distressed people. Vivekananda made his tour to the West to repair his broken health in 1899 A.D. In 1900 A.D. the Parliament of religion was again held in Paris of France. At that time he received the call of representing Hindu religion and he gave a lecture there. The foreign audience were overwhelmed by the lecture. He returned after a time but his health didn't improve any more. He died in 4th of July, 1902 after taking classes at Belur. After his death Tagore commented, that he wanted to blend both Eastern and Western culture, and sacrificed his whole life to fulfil his own thought so that there could be the interchange of ideas and thought of both the worlds. He devoted himself for the poor. His achievement lies in rousing respect for Indian religion, culture and people in the minds of the people of the world, though at the same time he remained tolerant of all religions. The teachings of the great monk that the only way to serve God is to serve His fellow men, should be remembered by all with great respect.

Chapter IX
Subhas Chandra Bose

Once there was a terrible bombing by the British forces at Burma. The soldiers of the Indian forces requested their leader to flee away for life. But the leader with a smile replied, "You are giving away your life for your motherland, Why not I, let we die together." Such a brave leader was our Netaji Subhas Chandra Bose.

He was born in a wealthy family on January 23, 1897 in the city of Cuttack of Orissa. His father Janakinath Basu was the well-known lawyer of Cuttack, though his ancestral home was in the village of Kodalia in 24-Pgs. His mother was Prabhabati Devi. His father believed that the future of their children lay in English education alone. But his mother however was of different temperament. The childhood of Subhas Chandra was influenced by his mother who was responsible for his great love for his motherland. She was the one who made him conscious of the great tradition of India.

After reading for years in European School, he was next admitted to Ravenshaw College. Then he was admitted to Presidency College at Kolkata. In Presidency College, he showed a great deal of courage by making an open revolt against the British Professor (Principal) Mr. F.E. Oaten when he made some bad remarks about the Indians in one of his lectures. As a result he was expelled from the college. This event highlights the fact that Subhas was very critical of the new Indian society which at the same time was a mixture of Indian and Western culture. However he passed his B.A. exam successfully from Scottish Church College.

In 1919, the 15th of September, Subhas went to Cambridge to fulfil the promise of his father to appear for the Indian Civil Service Examination. Though he did very well in the examination, he decided by that time that he would not serve in the Indian Civil Service under the British Government. He came back to India in 1921, to devote his life to the service of the country. Soon by the influence of C.R. Das, the great barrister as well as the leader of Mahatma Gandhi, he joined Congress. He was an active supporter of C.R. Das whose patriotic feeling for his country had a great impact on Subhas.

After joining the Indian National Congress, the first step taken by Subhas Chandra was to organise the boycott of the visit of the Prince of Wales to India in 1921. He was arrrested for such offence. After his release, Subhas engaged himself in relief work as Bengal was affected by severe flood during these days. When he was in jail, C.R. Das and Pandit Matilal Nehru formed "Swarajya Party" so that the Freedom movement never lost its impact. Subhas joined "Swarajya Party" and was the secretary and later on the Chief Executive Officer in Kolkata Corporation.

In 1925, Subhas experienced a shock due to the death of C.R. Das. Earlier in October 1924, Subhas was arrested on the charge of conspiracy and was sent to Mandalay jail in Burma. But he was released in May 1927 on health grounds. The death of C.R. Das weakened the Swaraj movement to such an extent that soon afterwards the Indian National Congress started formulating new policies to increase the pressure on the British to grant swaraj to India. The British also appointed the Simon Commission without any Indian member in it, resulting in the appeal by the Congress to boycott such commission. After the publication of the

Simon Commission's Report, the Congress appointed a committee, the Nehru Committee, headed by Motilal Nehru to frame the future constitution of India. In the fifth session of the All India Congress held in December, 1928, this report was submitted by Motilal Nehru to ask for the minimum political demand of the Indian people. It was at this session, Subhas organised a group of youth trained on military lines to maintain order at the location where Congress session was held and Subhas himself became the general officer commanding the volunteers.

A few months after, Subhas was elected as the President of All India Trade Union Congress. Because of his leadership abilities he was elected as Mayor of Kolkata in 1930. In 1932 Subhas went to Vienna for receiving medical treatment, Then he met Vithal Bhai Patel and together they issued a manifesto where they concluded that India would not be free until they had support from foreign countries ; however they totally disagreed with the views of Gandhiji in their manifesto. Its basis idea was to give up non-cooperation movement in a non-violent way and to take up the freedom struggle in a more aggressive way.

In 1934, Subhas Chandra had to return to see his dying father without the permission of the British Government, therefore he was interned at home. In 1934, he visited different places of Europe and made contact with many political leaders. He was elected the President of the Indian National Congress in January 1938, when he was abroad. He returned to India in the same year to preside over the 51st National Congress Session at Haripura in Gujarat. When his term of office began to come to an end, he expressed his desire to try for re-election as the President of the Congress but Gandhiji didn't approve of it. Subhas contested against the wishes of Gandhiji and was re-elected as the president of the Indian National Congress for a second time.

But because of the sharp difference between Gandhiji and Subhas, Subhas resigned from the post of President and after his resignation formed the Forward Block in 1939 to offer stiff resistance to the non-violence policy of the Congress party.

However when the Second World War took place Subhas Chandra, with the help of his Forward Block started strong anti-British movement throughout India. As a result he was imprisoned in July 1940. After a threat from Subhas, that he could go to indifinite hunger strike if not released immediately, he was released by the British Government but he was kept confined at home. But, Subhas Chandra, disobeying the British order, disappeared in disguise from his house. After leaving India in 1941, Subhas went to Germany as it had made war against the British. When Germany's defeat in war was quite imminent after the battle of Stalingrad, Subhas left Germany and went to South East Asia. Before his arrival in South East Asia Rashbehari Basu a well-known revolutionary believed in Subhas's Indian Army but another group, the Independence of India League, in South East Asia headed by Captain Mohan Singh, though had often difference of ideologies with that of Rashbehari Basu had equal respect for Subhas Chandra. Subhas then went to Singapore and was elected the leader of the freedom movement. Subhas Chandra maintained the two groups the Indian National Army and the Indian Independence League but throughly organised his forces to make war against the British. So the Indian National Army under the leadership of Subhas Chandra, made their war against the British in 1944, on the Arakan Front and next they crossed Burma border, but when the army came to Imphal, they were stopped by the British forces. Again heavy rain and the lack of supply for the Indian National Army made the army stop back and Subhas Chandra ordered for the retreat of the forces. When Subhas reached Bangkok, in May 1945, Germany had accepted defeat. After some time, Japan also gave up fighting, when its two cities Hiroshima and Nagasaki were destroyed by the bombing of America. So it was not possible for the Indian National Army to continue their fighting any more against the British, having received no help from any where. Then on August 17, 1945, Subhas Chandra took a plane from Saigon. But after five days, it was announced by Tokyo Radio that the Plane in which he was travelling had an aircrash. The Indian National Army soon surrendered to the British. From thereon Subhas Chandra was never seen or heard of again.

Subhas Chandra, the great leader of India-tried his best to free India from the tyrancy of the British. Today his dream has come true. India is free but he is no more with us to live in free India.

Chapter X

Dr. Bidhan Chandra Roy

A selfconfident and dutiful man once said that he believed that the Bengalees would gain a worthy place in the world with the help of their intelligence and strength. So every Bengalee should work to the utmost throughout his life.

In 1882 A.D., on the 1st of July-Bidhan Chandra was born in Bakipur at Patna. His father was Prakash Chandra and his mother's name was Agore Kamini Devi. His nick name was Bhajan, given by his grandmother. At the age of fourteen, Bidhan Chandra's mother died. Among the three brothers, Bidhan Chandra was the youngest. His elder brother Subadh Chandra was a barrister and his second brother Sadhan Chandra was an engineer. The three brothers were awarded high degrees and did good service in their own country. Subashini and Sarojini were the two sisters of Bidhan Chandra. In his childhood, Bidhan Chandra was educated at Patna. In his student life he passed his examination as an ordinary student.

He didn't make any remarkable result in Entrance Examination, neither in F.A. or B.A. Exam. In 1901 A.D., he started reading medicine in the Medical College. While reading medicine, he was in financial trouble but he had great attention in study. As he had financial trouble, so his father gave him the opportunity of working for twelve hours as a male nurse in the house of a rich patient on the salary of Rs.8. The Vice-principal of Medical College Colonel Lukis liked him very much. With his cooperation he passed LMS exam. After passing medical examination, he got service in Medical College. But on advice of Colonel Lukis he went to England to study medicine. Having reached there, he at first was in great trouble. In England he did not get seat in the college. Still he never gave up hope. Dr. Shore was the head of the best Medical Institute of England. Bidhan Chandra repeatedly met Mr. Shore. Dr. Shore at first didn't help him but at last he was overwhelmed by his eagerness and ordered him to get admission in his college. With help of his intelligence and merit, he was awarded the highest degree like M.R.C.P. and F.R.C.S. in the same year and came back to his won country in 1911 A.D. When his father died, he started his career by engaging himself in Government service. After some time, he on his own initiative started practising in medicine. At that time he started teaching in Car Michael College at Kolkata. Asutosh Mukherjee told him to become the Senate member of the Kolkata University. In 1916 A.D., he became the fellow of the Senate of the University. He looked after the improvement of the University. He had a great foresight. Apart from that, he was also very hard working. It is also said that before earning money on private practices, he even tried his luck as a part-time driver. He also established pathological laboratory in his own house to earn money. Though he never shone in medical profession at the beginning in a short time his medical practice flourished. He was regarded one of the famous doctors. He got so much regard as a doctor, that the people used to regard him as God being so much benefited by his medicine.

Bidhan Chandra also had great love for his country. In 1920 A.D., he first joined in Congress. Then he supported Deshbandhu Chittaranjan and joined in Freedom Movement. As a result he was imprisoned by the English. At that time, he used to supervise the patients of the Alipore Central Jail.

After being released from jail (which was before the scheduled time) he became the Mayor of Calcutta Corporation. Being in the post of a Mayor, he looked after the improvement of Kolkata. In 1941, he became the Vice Chancellor of Kolkata University and showed a great deal of efficiency in such work. When in 1947, our country became independent at that time he was in America for the treatment of his eye, That year in the month of November, he came back to his own country. After his return, he found that his most beloved native land was divided into two and was full of troubles. He tried actively to solve the problem of the distressed refugees coming up from East Bengal. In the year 1948, he got an opportunity and became the Chief Minister of the problematic West Bengal and he was in the post throughout his life. Being the Chief Minister, he looked after the maximum development of West Bengal. As a result at present, some renowned places of West Bengal, like Durgapur, Digha, Kalyani came into existence.

The education and industry of West Bengal made enormous development by his own initiative. His sense of duty, firm determination were great. In spite of his participation in politics, he never gave up his profession of medicine. Even when he was the Chief Minister he daily used to see his patients for some time freely, without taking any fees. He did not feel tired in this kind of activity. Today the development of West Bengal in the field of education and industry in India, were due to his own active help.

In 1962, the 1st of July, he died. He was really an out and out Bengalee. He showed a great deal of respect for his country and the nation—so he was a great personality and popular to all. All great people like Motilal Nehru, Mahatma Gandhi, Jawaharlal Nehru, Indira Gandhi were benefitted by his treatment. When Mahatma, made hunger strike, Bidhan Roy was by his side. At one time when Gandhiji was leading an imprisoned life, gradually giving up all the medicines to be on death bed, Bidhan Roy requested him to take one medicine. At first Gandhi, refused but he had agreed to take medicine on his advice as Dr Roy made him convince that though it was possible for him to treat all people freely but he had treated a person who was the representative of 40 million people.

The relation before Nehru and Bidhan Roy was very cordial in spite of the fact that they had some differences of opinion. At one time Nehru wrote to him, "What is the problem which you face, in Bengal ?" Bidhan Roy wrote to him, "Bengal is suffering from the problem of food, employment and lodging", to solve such problem.

He had no conjugal life but to him work was worship. With the dint of his genius, boundless love for common people, and tireless efforts, he was capable of winning the love of countless people of his country. His motto in life was, "You must try to perform anyhing according to your ability and for the rest you have to depend on God." In his view, one should not sit idle rather one should try hard even if one may not be successful in his endeavour.

Chapter XI

Jagadish Chandra Bose

Once a boy of a rich family was admitted to a school at Faridpur. He was very simple yet bright and intelligent. Even his nature was very sweet. But for one reason every student tried to avoid him. He always used to ask them, "Well, can you tell me what is the name of that tree ? What is the name of that creeper ? "How did they grow ? How did they live ?" etc. His companions used to laugh and said, "The boy was mad." The name of that boy was Acherya Jagadish Chandra Basu, the famous scientist. Mymansingh, now in Bangladesh, in November 30, 1858 was the birth-place of Jagadish Chandra Basu. His ancestral home was in the village Rarrikhal, Dacca district. His father was Bhagaban Chandra Basu who was a Deputy Magistrate at Faridpur and his mother's name was Bamasundari Devi.

Jagadish Chandra was brought up in a home steeped in Indian tradition and culture. The king Karna of the *Mahabharata* who struggled through out his life to achieve success inspired him. He thus believed that true success is born out of defect. Jagadish Chandra after getting his admission in a village school had to mix with the boys of different classes but he didn't hesitate to mix with them. After completing his education at his village- school, he was sent to Hare School at Kolkata, He passed his Entrance Examination from Hare School and was admitted to St. Xavier's School at Kolkata. There he found himself among the Europeans and Anglo-Indian boys. They were amused to have among them a village boy. One of them was a champion boxer, who tried to bully young Jagadish. One day Jagadish, unable to tolerate took up the challenge and somehow won in the fight. In this way, he gained the respect of his classmates. Thereafter no one dared to tease him.

While reading in the college, his aim was to become a doctor. But his mission was not fulfilled. Jagadish Chandra being also a great hunter, was once invited by one of his father's friends to go to Assam for hunting. But he was late in arriving the actual place. Without taking any rest, he went straight to the hunting spot. Then he began to wait along with other hunters for their prey. Suddenly a sound was heard. All at once, Jagadish Chandra, thinking it to be some animal shot his bullet. But in stead of an animal, it was found that his bullet hit a tree. He felt as if the tree was bleeding very much. Immediately he started to nurse it. He spent a sleepless night always thinking about the wounded tree. Next day he was so sick that he had to come to Kolkata for treatment but he was not completely cured.

In spite of his sickness, he went to England to become a doctor. But he couldn't continue his study—because of his illness. At last he started studying Physics, Chemistry and Natural Science at Christ Church College. In 1885, he returned from abroad with a B.Sc. degree and passed Natural Science Tripos. He was offered a lectureship at Presidency College in Kolkata on a salary half than that of his "white" colleagues. He accepted the job but refused to draw his salary as a protest. After three years, when the college principal, a Briton, found him to be a brilliant teacher, he conceded his demand. He was paid full salary from the date he joined the college.

At that time, the research laboratory of the college was not good. But Jagadish Bose though he didn't get any help from the government of the time, to improve the laboratory, tried on his own expenses, to employ some skilled mechanics to make some scientific instruments for the research work. Then he began to make his research work on radio waves. He was rightly regarded as the inventor of wireless telegraphy. In 1895, a year before GuglieImo, Marconi patented this invention, so he received the honour of making such invention though Jagadish Bose demonstrated its functioning in public.

In 1897, he started doing research work on whether the plants have got life. He came to the conclusion that the plants have life. Just as the part of the body feels pain, so also plants feel pain, though they don't have brain. But there are an small cells in them behaving in the same manner like that of an animal. Then he went to England to show before the members of the Royal Society his experiment on plants. He gained a great deal of praise for his research work. His lecture, earlier withheld, was published, circulated all over the world. He was elected Fellow of the Royal Society in 1920. He also invented several sensitive instruments. The most wonderful was Crescograph, an instrument to measure the rate of the growth of a plant. Even the Government of India gave him the title "Sir".

The Bose Institute at Kolkata which he founded on his own expense, mainly deals with the study of plants and also other research works are going on in this institute. Though he was a great scientist, he had also a great love for literature. He wrote some articles on science which were published in bulk called "Abaktya". He was also a great patriot and spent his money for the welfare of his peaple, Because of his love for his country he expressed his wish to Tagore that he wouldn't mind if he was to take his birth in India for hundred of times. The great scientist died in 23rd November, 1937. We should pay our homage to the great scientist who was not a person to accept any kind of defeat but to fight against odds right from his childhood.

Chapter XII

Meghnad Saha

In 1905, a great revolution began when the Britrish wanted to divide Bengal into East and West. People couldn't accept such injustice. A boy specially had felt in his mind the wrongs of the British Government but was too young to protest against it. The boy was Meghnad Saha, the famous scientist of Bengal. But he wanted to make protest in an indirect way. His opportunity came when the Britsh Governer of Bengal visited his school. Despite the stern warning that everyone should be present before the Governor he and some of his friends on that day as a work of protest, didn't go to their school but later on were severely punished for their doings. Their names were as a result struck off the roll. Beside Meghnad Saha couldn't further enjoy the scholership which he was awarded a few months before. In fact, he showed such spirit of patriotisn all through his life. So he not only had great contributions in the field of science but also fought much for the service of his motherland. He not only tried to raise the status of science in independent India, but also served the cause of the poor.

Meghnad Saha was born in Seoratali of Dacca district now in Bangladesh in 1893. His father Jagannath Saha was nothing more than a poor humble grocer and his mother was Bhubaneswari Devi. His father could barely manage to keep his large family from starvation. He wanted Meghnad his fifth son to earn for his family even when he was a child. But according to the advice of some teachers,

Meghnad's father got the child admitted to a boarding school, eleven kilometers from the village with a well wisher paying his tuition fees and other charges.

Simply through merit and hard labour Meghnad Saha won a schlarship to go to Dacca for higher education. After the boycott, as mentioned above he had to join another school. However in the final examination he stood first. Again winning a scholarship he joined Presidency College Kolkata. Here he was not only taught by eminent teachers like J.C. Bose and P.C. Ray but had brilliant contemporaries like S.N. Bose and P.C. Mahalanobis. He stood second in B.Sc. and also in M.SC, in order of merit. He wanted to join the Indian Finance Service, but his earlier disrespect to the Government at the school and his close friendship with the great patriot Subhas Chandra Bose stood in his way and he couldn't accept any kind of job under the British Government. So he started doing research work in Physics and Mathematics and earned his living by teaching some students. In 1917 he got appointment as a lecturer at the newly opened University College of science in Kolkata. Thermodynamics, relativity and atomic theories, the latest developments in physics and the books on the subjects were read by Saha largely and could teach them as well. While studying he made the solution of the problem of Astrophysics—which deals with the nature of the stars, their temperature and internal structure and composition. Just as sunlight passing through suspended raindrops produces the rainbow, a band of colours called "spectrum" is produced when sunlight passes through a glass-made solid transparent object called glass prism. He knew physics quite well and therefore invented ionisation formula, which explained the presence of the spectral lines. The formula enabled an astronomer to know the temperature, pressure and other aspects of the interior of the sun or any other star. The scientific world applauded his work and his work took him to the peak of glory. In 1927, almost a decade after his discovery, Saha was elected fellow of the

Royal Society. But some of the scientists didn't accept his formula and even prevented him from joining the Physics department of Allahabad University. But however they were not successful in his efforts. He didn't care what others said of him and because of his tenacity of purpose went on doing his research and teaching.

In Allahabad, he began research work in spectroscopy the study of the spectrum (images formed when a beam of radiant energy is subjected to dispersion) and ionosphere (radio waves are transmitted to great distances around the earth) and thus raised the department to international status. On his own initiative, nuclear physics was taught for the first time at Kolkata University. In 1948, he founded the Saha Institute of Nuclear Physics at Kolkata.

Not only as a scientist, Saha was also a great social worker. Since he himself was poor, the poverty of his own countrymen was known to him. During the time of the partition of Bengal, when many refugees came from East Bengal (now Bangladesh) he took active steps to solve their problems and to resettle them. He also did not forget the relief work he had done in his childhood when the river near his house used to overflow its bank duing the monsoon. He studied the origin and control of floods and suggested a number of river valley projects. The Damoder Valley, Bhakra-Nangal and Hirakud projects are the final products of work that he started.

Saha was fearless and frank in his criticism of some government policies. He had full faith in industrialisation and was against the village movement which he claimed, would not solve the problem of poverty, disease and ignorance. He founded a magazine 'Science and Culture' and expressed his own views with the help of his magazine. In 1952, he stood as an independent candidate for Parliament and was elected by a wide margin. He died in February 16, 1956. All the scientists of India as well as his country people owe to him much for his great contributions in the field of science.

Chapter XIII
Surendranath Banerjee

Once a small boy came to his village school late. The teacher got angry and scolded him for his being so late. The boy felt so much insulted that next day he didn't want to go to school. That little boy later on became Surendranath Banerjee.

He was born in 10th November 1848 A.D. Though he was born in a rich family he had to lead a very simple life from his childhood days. Though his father was a well known doctor, Surendranath at first was educated in a village school and then a Bengali medium school. His real student life began at Parental Academic Institution. In order to converse with the Anglo-Indian students, he only by his own efforts, learnt English. However he passed his B.A. from Kolkata University and then was sent to England to sit for Civil Service Examination. In 1869, he passed Indian Civil Service Exam with success. When he came back to his own country he was appointed as the Assistant Magistrate of Srihatta. But because of some differences with the British Government, he was expelled from Civil Service. Even the expulsion, didn't stand in the way of his becoming a barrister. In such a condition Surendranath felt that as he was an Indian, he was given so much troubles by the British. He also felt for the other Indians whose conditions he feared, would be the same like him. Then he decided to fight against such injustices of the British on the Indians. Returning to Kolkata he at the same time tried to find out a job for himself but he couldn't. At that time, he gave a lecture in a meeting as how to remove darkness from the society. Hearing his wonderful speeches, the students were greatly pleased. Soon Iswar Chandra asked him to become the professor of English of Metropolitan College and he accepted the job. This gave him the opportunity to become more closely associated with the students. He became the active member of the Student's Association and inspired the students so that they might feel for their motherland. Besides as he had wonderful power of speaking, he was invited from many places to give lectures on several subjects. He also spoke on the usefulness of English education. Later on, he became the lecturer of City college so that he could easily get an opportunity of mixing himself up with the students.

In fact he was never tired of doing any kind of work and always did his works well. He himself set up, with the help of Ananda Mahan Basu the Indian Associaton to spread its activities throughout India. There was a plan of establishing Bengal Association by Pandit Iswarchandra Vidyasagar and others. But Surendranath wished that its field must spread throughout India, and after many arguments Surendranath's proposal was accepted. On the very day, when it was going to be established, Surendranath son died, Still he attended the meeting and made his speeches. Everybody present was charmed by his speeches. Such was his mental strength at the time of work, he never cared for his family. It was because of his untiring effort, Ripon college was established. In 1882, he was attached to a school named Presidency Institution. He made certain changes in it. At that time, Lord Ripon was the Govenor General of Bengal and it was named Ripon College on his permission. From 1875 to 1912 A.D. Surendranath remained in the job of teaching.

In 1856, Victoria, the Queen of England made an announcement when she instructed for the development of Indian Municipal institution. Surendranath felt that the improvement of such institution was the first step towards self-governed education. So he made his country people educated in politics and self-controlled government. To carry on such agitation, he took the responsibility of carrying on

"Bengali" a newspaper. In, the meantime, he was arrested for the time being in Presidency jail in a case. Being released he again engaged himself for the service of the country. In 1886, in the first conference of the National Congress at Kolkata, Surendranath proposed for the reform of administration other wise to carry on agitation on such issue. In 1887, in the Congress meeting at Madras, Surendranath Banerjee and some other were selected to go to England to receive the support of the people of England in their fight for freedom. In England he could easily win the hearts of the English people by his excellent power of speaking. In 1892, some reforms were made for Bengal legislative Assembly and he became the selected member of the Assembly. In 1885, he became the Chairman of Barrackpore Municipality. In 1895, he was elected the President of the annual meeting of National Congress at Pune and there he delivered a very attractive speech. In 1902, as the president of the National Congress session at Amedabad, he received warm welcome from the people of Amedabad. Lord Curzon as a Governor of India felt that the Indians were becoming united against the foreign rule. So he tried to divide Bengal to make it less powerful. The people of India made an active revolt and Surendranath took initiative to lead such agitation. On the other hand the leaders of Congress Party developed difference of opinion among themselves regarding their strategy of how to oppose the British Government ; so in 1918, Surendranath had to leave Congress party. But still he didn't give up serving his country people. British government also made certain reforms in the administration of India and Montagu Chamesford reforms were introduced. Surendranath and his group accepted such reforms. In 1920, he was awarded the title "Sir" by Indian Government. Even after his death, he is still alive in our mind. It is after his name, Ripon College, set up by him was named Surendranath College in 1948-49. Surendranath as a leader of our country will receive due respect and honour for all the time because of his relentless struggle against British imperialism.

Chapter XIV

Ashutosh Mukherjee

In 1864 of the 29th of June, Ashutosh Mukherjee was born in Malanga Lane of Bowbazar, Kolkata. His father's name was Gangaprasad and his mother was Jagattarini Devi. Gaugaprasad from his very childhood tried his best to bring up Asutosh in such a way so that he could became a man with all round personality. The medical chamber of Gangaprasad was at Bowbazar. There Ashutosh used to go and notice how his father used to give various coloured medicines to his patients. So Ashutosh was inspired and pretended to become a doctor. He used to fill up some vacant containers with water by sitting by the side of a pond. But once suddenly by accident, while doing that, he slipped and fell into the water. One of the assistants of the doctor, passing by the road lifted the child from the water.

After finishing his primary education at home, his father got him admitted in a children's school. From his childhood he was a boy of great merit. So within two years, he completed the syllabus which the children used to complete in six years.

In stead of getting him admitted in any English medium school, his father made arrangement for him to be educated at home and engaged some tutors for his education. He was never seen to be scolded for his learning his daily lessons. Beside he had a wonderfal memory ; so he could easily master different subjects specially mathematics with a great deal of proficiency. In fact he had so much interest in study, that it was feared that he would be sick at any time because of continuous hard labour and strain. Once he was locked up by his parents without having any pen pencil or paper for study. But Ashutosh with the help of a charcoal which he found in the room, worked out sums on the floor of the room.

At the age of ten, because of his serious illness he was sent to Mathura by his father in his friend's house for the change of climate. After sufficient rest and food, he became well. On his way back from Mathura, he was acquinted with Vidyasagar in the station Mogolsharai, who presented him a book named *Rabinson Crusoe*. After his return from Mathura, he was admitted to Bhawanipur South Subarbon School. Sibnath Shastri was the headmaster of the school. He was admitted to class IV (at present class VII standard). As he had great interest in Mathematics he loved to read *Dharapat* and his father employed an able teacher for helping him in his study. While reading in class IV he could easily solve the problems of Algebra. From his childhood he was taught by his father, how to deliver a lecture as he had great ambition to become a judge of high court. He was advised by his father, to deal with his school lessons in the pose of a lecture. He also learnt Sanskrit grammar, dramas and poems from a pandit called Panchanon Paldhi. Besides school books, he used to read many good books. He memorised the first part of Milton's Paradise Lost after being promoted to third class standard (equivalent to class VIII). He also translated into English *Kathamala, Akhyanmanjari, Bodhodoy* etc. When he was promoted to class II standard (equivalent to at present class IX) he had already solved Geometry of Euclid. He liked great epics *The Ramayana, The Mahabharata,* also the books written by Vidyasagar for the improvement of his mind. Passing the Entrance Examination successfully, he was admitted to Presidency College in the first year. At first he couldn't mix up freely with his friends as he had no habit of doing so. However he was liked by W. Buth, the professor of Mathematics for his love of Mathematics. As he was dressed in plain, he used to call him "simple man" out of love for him. He used to spend his leisure time in the library, reading different types of magazines. In the library, he solved the sums of M.A. and at home studied learning French and Latin language on his own initiative. He was also eager to learn English literature, Sanskrit, History, Science. In the first year class, English grammar was taught by Professor Robson. Once it so happened that Ashtosh could easily make exact translation of the ancient tales of Greece as told by the professor. Later on the professor could easily detect and appriciate that it was because of his excellent memory it was possible for Ashutosh to do it, though he was advised to write anything in his own language.

Though Ashutosh had great eagerness for study, he knew that his father wouldn't allow him to sit up late at night for study. So he had to do it secretly without the knowledge of his father. One day when his father came to know about it, he didn't allow his son to do it any further. But because of late-night study, his health was affected. Despite it he passed FA exam successfully. Before the result of FA, he got admission in B.A. and showed great proficiency in Mathematics which was taught by W. Buth. He in his first class taught seventyfive pages of a Mathematics book at a stretch within an hour but Ashutosh because of his merit had no difficulty, in understanding it and besides he had already read the book. In 1884 he stood first in B.A. and in 1885, he stood first in MA and was awarded a gold medal. He also started reading law in the C.T. College sometime before, and at the same time he studied Philosophy and difficult books on Mathematics. He also secured stipend of Premchand, Raychand Exam and got Rs.10,000 as a reward and at the age of twentythree was appointed as an examiner of Mathematics exam. After passing law in 1888, he started doing practice at Calcutta High Court in the month of August and in 1890 was give the title 'Doctor of Law', having passed Hons. in Law. At the age of twentyfour he became the Member of University Syndicate. In 1908, he founded Calcutta Mathematical Society. In 1898, he was appointed as a law professor and started delivering lectures on law to the students throughout the year and in 1904 he acquired his much desired post of becoming the Judge of Kolkata High Court.

While he applied for the permission of doing M.A. in science (which was permitted by the University) he was married to Jogomaya Devi, the daughter of Ramnarayan Bhattacharjee, the pandit of Krishnagar. He had great love for his mother. Once Lord Curzon on some urgent business wanted to send Ashutosh along with the distinguished guests to London. But he refused to obey his order unless his mother gave him the permission to do so.

In fact his personality was really great. Once on his return to Kolkata, by train, there was a military English man and nobody else was there. At that time, the British people used to hate the Indians as natives. The Saheb from the very beginning felt discomfort at the sight of a Bengalee. Within a little time, Ashutosh went to sleep after putting off his shoes, and lifting his legs on the table. In the mean time the English man felt disgusted at such a sight and threw off his shoes from the train. So when Ashutosh awoke, he could easily understand who had done the job, but he remained silent. When Saheb went to sleep, he (Ashutosh) on the other hand threw off the coat which was beside the Saheb through the window of the train. When the Saheb awoke and searched for his coat, Ashutosh shortly replied, "Your coat has gone to search for my shoes." The Saheb got angry but kept mumb in the presence of Ashutosh's strong personality.

Ashutosh had also great love for his country. Once at Mysore when he had gone for the spread of education, the king invited him to a feast. There he went in his own national dress which was also accepted by the king who honoured him for his strong personality and his love for his country, though it was the custom prevalent, to go to the king's palace by wearing a turban.

He (Ashutosh) had a great contribution for the spread of Bengali language. Because of his initiative, the course in M.A. in Bengali language was introduced. He got the post of Vice Chancellor of Kolkata University. He was awarded the title 'Knight' by the king of India for his great contribution for the spread of education. After his retirement, he again started his practice in law. After a time, he had to go to Patna on an urgent piece of business. There he died in the 25th of May, 1924.

Chapter XV

Sibnath Shastri

A boy of thirteen or fourteen was very much fond of catching birds and keeping them as pets to the total dislike of his father. One day he was going to some place, accompanied by his father. His father advanced a bit. The boy suddenly found a bird on the tree. He knew the habit of the bird *i.e.* if it is absent minded, it would fall down if one throws a stone, aiming at its leg. The boy did it, quite unnoticed by his father. Suddenly the bird fell down in front of his father's feet. His father nursed it and gave it away to a stranger, totally unaware that his son had done it. The boy also had a trick to catch the birds. When the two birds were quarreling with each other, on the branch of the tree, he used to spread out a cloth on his lap and the birds while quarreling ultimately used to fall on his lap. Sometimes he used to steal the small birds from their nests and after making a hole on a bowl often kept them as his pets by making an artificial nest in the bowl. Sometimes he used to feed those birds with grasshoppers, by hunting them from the fields. He was also very curious to know the reason of everything that was happening around. The boy was Shibnath Shastri.

He was born in the village Changripota in the 31st of January 1847. After six months, his mother took him to his father-in-laws' house, Mogilpur. His father, Harananda Bhattacharjee was the student of Sanskrit College during the time. He (Sibnath) was taken care of by his great grandfather and an attendant as he had lost his grand-father at an young age. At the age of five, his mother admitted him to a local 'Pathshala'. She herself took care of her son's education. After a time he was admitted to Hardinge Model School. There he used to study 'Barnamala' and 'Shishushikha' published by the School Book Society.

In those days, it was the custom of the Brahmin pandit's house to offer food to their ancestral God before having them as their own. But Sibnath at the age of four or five was adamant that he would not take such kind of food ; so his food had to be kept separately. But he loved very much his own sister Unmadini who was born when he was six years of age and took a great care of her. But his mother had full control over her son Sibnath. Once due to the influence of bad boys, he used abusive language to his mother, so his mother gave him severe punishment.

After his Upanayan (a ritual of having a holi thread) his father took Sibnath to Kolkata by foot and he was admitted to Sanskrit College where the principal was Vidyasagar. After staying at several places, he stayed with his maternal uncle's house. There due to some bad company he started smoking 'hookah'. But by the advice of his maternal uncle, he gave up such habit. After his marriage with Prasannamoyee the daughter of Nabin Chandra Chakraborty of Raipur, he went back to Kolkata for education. He stayed at Kolkata at many places to carry on his education but at Bhawanipur in the house of Mahesh Choudhury, he really got a suitable place for study, though he was engaged there in the task of store keeping. He not only was happy to have a suitable environment there but also he was also enthusiastic about his study as he was acquainted with a huge number of books there. Gradually he became attached to Brahmasamaj and started writing poems in the newspaper 'Somprakash' and 'Education Gazette'. He also started going to Brahmasamaj at Bhawanipur for meditation of God. He used to go to his own village on summar, or puja vaccation and at that time he was to worship their ancestral God. But to control his ownself he stopped doing that and restrained himself from taking meat. Because of his perseverance and his concentration, he stood second, having scored first class in Entrance Examination and was awarded a scholarship. In 1868, he was also awarded scholarship in LA Exam. He studied for LA Exam for two and half months for eighteen hours at a stretch. Regularly he, after returning from the college, used to read the life histories of the famous people from Bittns Biographical Dictionary. He also read the books of Theodore Parker, 'Essays written in the intervals of business' by Arthar Helps etc.

As Sibnath had the intention of becoming a lawyer, he decided to sit for B.L. examination after passing B.A. But after second thought he dropped such idea. Next he passed M.A. in 1872 and was given the title 'Shastri'.

After a time, he took the job of teaching in Keshab Sen's newly established girls' school and took the responsibility of being the editor of 'Somprakash' when his maternal uncle fell sick. In 1874, he became the headmaster of South Subarban School at Bhawanipur. Gradually he became involved in the movement of social reforms.

Besides preaching the main motto of Brahmasamaj, he also advocated the social and political harmony. As he was involved in various kinds of jobs, it was not possible for him to continue his government service and he had to resign in 1878. In 1879, he established City School along with Surendranath Banerjee and Ananda Mohan Basu. He was also the editor of a magazine named 'Mukul'. He will be remembered in Bengali literature for his literary achievements like 'Mejo Bou' (a novel) 'Himadri Kusum' (a poetical work) etc.

Bihar

Chapter I

Krishna Singh

Sri Krishna Singh (21 October, 1887 - 31 January, 1961) known as Dr. S.K. Singh, Sri Babu and Bihar Kesari was the first Chief Minister of the Indian State of Bihar (1946-61). Along with the nationalists like Rajendra Prasad, Singh can be considered as one of the architects of Modern Bihar. Hemchandra Basu, the son of the Headmaster of Zila School and an advocate of Munger Court gave a very vivid description about Krishna Singh, "I distinctly remember, the occasion one day in 1916 .... I was highly pleased to see the charming young man .... now grown up to the stature of manhood, full of energy and promise, with a face radiant with intelligence and spirit." [Jha, Punil Kumar (2009) *Activities of Dr. Shri Krishna Singh in Provincial Politics* (1915-1947), Janaki Prakashan, Patna p. 238].

Singh was born on 21 October, 1887 in Khanwa in Nawada district of Bihar. His paternal village is Maur, near Barbigha in the then Munger District. His father was religious minded belonging to Brahmin family. His mother, an unassuming person died of plague when Singh was five years of age. He was educated in the village school and at Zila school in Munger. In 1906, he joined Patna college. Having studied law, he started practising in Munger. Within a short time he was married and had two sons also.

After doing graduation from Patna College, Sri Babu, completed his M.A. and B.L. doing well from Kolkata University. Next he joined the Munger District Bar as a lawyer on the 1st of April, 1916 and became gradually a rising lawer. He also did M.L. degree and joined the High Court at Patna. But suddenly he changed his mind, left his legal profession, to join Non-cooperation Movement of Mahatma Gandhi. At Munger he struggled hard to free India from the British rule. Though he was arrested for the first time in 1922, though Congress Seva Dal was declared illegal, he was known as Bihar Keshari by the people. Being released from jail in 1923, he became a member of All India Congress Committee in the same year. In 1927, he became the member of the Legislative Council and in 1929 became General Secretary of Bihar Pradesh Congress Committee. He had a vital role in the Namak Satyagrah at Garhpura in 1930. He was arrested for a short period and was again arrested for two years during Civil Disobedience Movement. After being released he started his nationalist work to work with the Kisan Sabha. After repeated arrests, he became a member of the Central Assembly in 1935. He occupied a central place in the Provincial Working Committee and of the Congress Organization in the state for thirty years. He enjoyed a great deal of popularity in the party and acted as a great coordinator between party and Government.

When Congress came to power, Sinha formed his Cabinet at Patna on July 20, 1937. Because of the difference of opinion between the Governor and him and his colleague Anugrah Narayan Sinha regarding the release of the political prisoners, he and his colleague resigned. When the Governor had to accede to their demands, they joined office. Then they again resigned on a different issue. However Krishna Singh was regarded one of the makers of modern Bihar. Singh served Bihar continuously from 1946 until his death on 31 January, 1961 at the age of 73. In 1978 , the Ministry of Culture established a science museum called Sri Krishna Science Centre. The biggest conference hall in Patna. Sri Krishna Hall is also named after him.

All the development projects needed for the state of Bihar, such as several river valley projects, the first five year plan period etc. were possible under the leadership of Shree Babu and A.N. Sinha. During the second five year plan period, Shri Babu brought forward several heavy industries like, Bokaro Steel Plant, Barauni Fertiliser Plant, Barauni Dairy Project etc. for the development of the state.

His (Shree Babu) contribution in the cultural and social development of the state was great. He established the Rajendra Chatra Niwas at Kolkata for Bihar students, Sanskrit College at Patna, Ravindra Bhavan at Patna etc. Sri Babu maintained good working relations with the Secretariat officials and gave protection to police from being demoralised because police in his opinion symbolised efficiency, service, protection and help to the people in stead of tyranny, domination, oppression. Caste had nothing to play in promotion, transfer, posting and in working relationship of police officials with ministers or the Chief Minister. Sri Babu had in fact the qualities of head and heart *e.g.* humanism, integrity and secularism. As a political figure he had absolute integrity.

Sri Babu, being a progressive leader, introduced substantive land reform laws at the early period of Bihar's history. However Sri Babu was in favour of the growth of agriculture and he wanted to do away with the constraints and hindrances in the way of the growth of productive forces in agriculture. Justice V.R. Krishna Iyer has commented, "Sri Krishna Singh, Govid Ballabh Pant, Bidhan Chandra Roy, ... E.M.S. Namboodiripad and others of that stature were heavy weights in their own right and brought into political administration a texture of nationalism, federalism, realism and even some touch of pragmatic socialism .... Sri Krishna lived poor, died poor and identified himself with the poor." (Kumar/principal editor), Dr. Vijay (2013), *Srikrishna Singh Smriti Granth, Vichar our Darshan,* Patna, Bihar State Archives.)

Chapter II

Dr. Rajendra Prasad

Dr. Rajendra Prasad (3 December 1884 - 28 February 1963) was the first President of the Republic of India. Rajendra Prasad was a Kayastha Hindu born in Zeradai, in the Siwan district of Bihar. His father Mahadev Sahai, earned proficiency both in the Sanskrit and Persian languages, while his mother, Kamleshwari Devi, was a religious minded woman who used to tell stories from the *Ramayana* to her son. At the age of five, he was given by his parents after the care of a Moulavi accomplished Muslim scholar, to learn the Persian language, Hindi and arithmatic. After completing his traditional elementery education, he was sent to the Chapra District School. Meanwhile he was married to Rajavanshi Devi at a tender age. He then with his elder brother Mahendra Prasad went to study at T.K. Ghosh's Academy in Patna for two years. He stood first in the Entrance Examination in the university of Kolkata and was awarded a scholarship of Rs. 30 per month. He joined Presidency College, Kolkata in 1902 as a science student. He passed Intermediate level classes, as F.A. under the University of Kolkata in March 1904 and took graduation degree with first division from there in March 1905. He was so intelligent that an examiner once commented on his answer sheet, "examinee is better than examiner." (Miglani Neha, 20 May, 2012) "Evaluators for preserving of lawless answer sheets." (The Times of India, 2015) Gradually he became interested in the study of arts and did his M.A. in Economics, securing first division from the University of Kolkata in December 1907.

It was due to his sense of duty towards his family and education, that he refused to join Servants of India Society. Prasad played the main role in the formation of the Bihari Students Conferences in 1906 in the hall of the Patna College. It was the first organisation of its kind in India, having some leaders from Bihar like Anugrah Narayan Sinha, Shri Krishna Singh and Shri Deep Narayan Singh.

Dr. Rajendra Prasad served in various educational institutions as a teacher. Having completed his M.A. in Economics, he became a professor of English at the Langat Singh College of Muzaffarpur in (Bihar) and went on to become the principal. Later on, he left it to study law. In 1909, while doing his law in Kolkata, he also worked as Professor of Economics at Kolkata City College. In 1915, appearing in the examination of Masters in Law, he passed the examination and was awarded a gold medal. He completed his doctorate degree in Law from Allahabad University in 1937.

In 1916, he joined the High Court of Bihar and Odisha. Later on, he became one of the first members of the Senate and Syndicate of the Patna University. He also practised law at Bhagalpur.

During Prasad's most initial association with Indian National Congress during 1906 annual session organised in Kolkata, he participated in as a volunteer, while studying in Kolkata. He joined the Indian National Congress in the year 1911, when annual session was again held in Kolkata. During the Lucknow session of Indian National Congress held in 1916, he met Mahatma Gandhi. He was so much charmed by the dedication, courage and conviction of Mahatma Gandhi, that as soon as the motion of Non cooperation was passed by Indian National Congress in 1920, he gave up his career as a lawyer, as well as his duties in the university, to join Non cooperation movement. He easily responded to the call of Gandhi to give up Western educational institution by asking his son Mrityunjaya Prasad to give up his studies there and to get admitted in Bihar Vidyapeeth, which he founded with his colleagues on traditional Indian model.

During the period of the independent movement, he came in association with Rahul Sanskrityayan, a writer, a knowledgeable person in different subjects. Rahul Sankrityayan regarded Prasad as a guide and teacher and was greatly attracted by Prasad's intellectual capacity. In many articles, he referred to his meeting with Sankrityayan and narrated about their meetings, He also wrote some articles for the revolutionary publications *Search light* and Desh and collected funds for these papers. He made a tour far and wide, giving lectures on the principles of the independence movement and explaning its significance.

Rajendra Prasad played an active role in helping the flood victims during the floods of 1914 that affected Bihar and Bengal. In 1934, when he was imprisoned, Bihar was hit by an earth quake. Even during the time, he passed on the relief work to his close colleague Anugrah Narayan Sinha. On release after two days, he set up Bihar Central Relief Committee on January 17, 1934. He himself took the responsibility of raising funds to render help to the people, affected by earthquake. During 31st May 1935 at the time of Quetta earth quake, he was forbidden to leave the country due to Government's order, then he set up Quetta Central Relief Committee in Sindh and Punjab under his own presidency.

Rajendra Prasad was elected the President of the Indian National Congress during the Bombay session in October 1934. He again became the president when Netaji Subhas Chandra Bose resigned in 1939. On August 8, 1942, Congress passed the Quit India Resolution in Bombay which led to the arrest of many Indian leaders. He was arrested from Sadagat Ashram, Patna and was sent to Bankipur central jail. After remaining imprisoned for nearly three years, he was released on 15 June 1945.

After the formation of Interim Government of 12 nominated ministers under the leadership of Jawaharlal Nehru, on 2 september 1996, he got the food and agricultural department. Later on he was elected the President of Constituent Assembly on 11th December 1946. Again on November 17, 1947, he became Congress President for the third time. Two and a half years after independence, on January 26, 1950 the Constitution of independent India was formally approved and Dr. Rajendra prasad was elected the the nation's first President.

Dr. Rajendra Prasad played an independent role in the field of politics. Following the tussle over the enactment of the Hindu Code Bill, he took an active part in state affairs. In 1962, after being a President for twelve years, he took a decision to retire. After giving up the office of the President of India or May 1962, he returned to Patna on May 14, 1962 and liked to stay in the campus of Bihar Vidyapeeth. He was honoured with the award the Bharat Ratna, the nation's highest civilian award. Rajendra Smriti Sangrahalaya in Patna is dedicated to him. His literary contributions are—*India Divided* (1946, on line), *Atmakatha* (1946) his autobiography written during his 3 year prison term in Bankipur Jail, *Mahatma Gandhi and Bihar Some Reminisences* (1949), *Since Independence* (published in 1960) etc. He expired on February 28, 1963. Apart from his literary contributions, his great love and dedication for his mother country made him a promiment figure in the world of politics.

Chapter III
Jayaprakash Narayan

Jaya Prakash Narayan (Harsu Dayal Srivastava) (11 October 1902 - 8 October 1979) is populerly known as JP or Lok Nayak (Hindi for **The People's Hero**). He was an Indian Independence activist, social reformer and political leader was born in 11 October in the village of **Sitabdiara** in Saran district of Bihar, India.

He hailed from a Kayastha family, being the fourth child of Harsu Dayal Srivastava and Phul Rani Devi. His father Harsu Dayal was a junior official in the Canal Department of the state government and had often a tour in the region. At the age of nine he left his village to enlist himself in the 7th class of the Collegiate School at Patna. At the time of his study in school, Jayaprakash read magazines like *Saraswati, Prabha* and *Pratap,* books like *Bharat-Bharati,* poems by Maithilsharan Gupta and Bharatendu Harishchandra, describing the courage and valour of the Rajput kings. Jayaprakash was also well acquinted with Bhagwad Gita. He proved himself to be a student of merit in school; his essay "The present State of Hindi in Bihar," won the best essay award. After the completion of his school life he appeared at the 'State Public Matriculation Examination' and was awarded a District merit scholarship to Patna College. In October 1920, Narayan was married to Prabhavati Devi, Braj Kishore Prasad's daughter, herself being a freedom fighter in her ownway. After their wedding, while Narayan was working at Patna, on invitation by Gandhi, Prabhavati became an inmate at the Ashram of Gandhi.

Once Jayaprakash, accompanied by some of his friends went to listen to Maulana Abul Kalam Azad, speaking about Non-cooperation movement launched by Gandhi, against the passing of the Rowlatt Act of 1919. Being a brilliant orator, his call to give up English education impressed so much Jayaprakash, that "he was swept away and momentarily lifted up to the skies." So Jayaprakash took Maulana's words to heart and left Patna college with just 20 days remaining for his examinations. He joined the Bihar Vidyapeeth a college run by the Congress.

After finishing up his courses at Vidyapeeth Jayaprakash decided to continue studies in the United States. At the age of twenty, Jayapraksh sailed abroad as Prabhavati stayed at Sabarmati. Jayaprakash reached California on Ocotober 8, 1922 and was admitted to Berkeley in January 1923. To continue his education Jayaprakash had to perform many menial jobs like picking up grapes, to dry them, packing fruits at a canning factory, washing dishes, working as a mechanic at a garage and at a slaughter house etc. So he was quite aware of the difficulties of the working class by doing all these jobs. Jayaprakash was forced to transfer to Iowa State when fees at Berkeley doubled. He was to transfer to many universities after that. He continued his favourite subject sociology and got much help from Professor Edward Ross, the father of sociology. In Wisconsin, Jayaprakash was aquainted with Karl Marx's *Das Kapital.* Because of the success of the Russian revolution of 1917, Jayaprakash came to the conclusion that Marxism was the only means to remove the suffering of the common people. His paper on Sociology, "Social Variation" was declared as the best of the year.

Narayan returned from US to India in late 1929 as a Marxist. He joined the Indian National Congress on the invitation of Jawaharlal Nehru in 1929. Mahatma Gandhi played the role of his mentor in the Congress. He shared a house at Kadam Kuan in Patna with his close friend and nationalist Ganga Sharan Sinha, with whom he had a very close relationship.

During the Indian independence movement he was imprisoned and tortured many times by the British. His role was very prominent during Quit India movement. After his jail in 1932 for civil disobedience against the British rule, Narayan was imprisoned again in Nasik jail, where he met Ram Monohar Lohia, Minoo Masani, Asok Mehta and other national leaders. After his release, the Congress Socialist Party, a leftwing group within the Congress was formed with Acharya Narendra Deva as President and Narayan as General Secretary. When Mahatma Gandhi started the Quit India Movement in August 1942, Jogendra Shukla sealed Hazaribagh central jail with Jayaprakash Narayan, Suraj Narayan Singh, Gulab Chand Gupta, Ramnandan Mishra, etc. to start underground movement for freedom.

Narayan became a prominent figure in State politics in the late 1960s. During 1974, a year of high inflation, unemployment and lack of supply of essential commodities, Nav Nirman Andolan movement of Gujrat asked Jayaprakash to have a peaceful agitation. On 8 April 1974, aged 72, he led a silent procession at Patna. The procession was lathi charged. On 5 June 1974, Jayaprakash addressed a large crowd at Gandhi Maidan at Patna. He declared boldly that as his country people after 27 years of freedom, were still oppressed by hunger, rising price, corruption, injustice, there was an urgency for Total Revolution. In 1974, he also took the lead in the students' movement in the state of Bihar, gradually developed into a popular people's movement, known as the Bihar movement. During such movement, J.P. gave a call for peaceful Total Revolution. Along with V.M. Tarkunde he founded the citizens for Democracy in 1974 and the People's Union for Civil Liberties in 1976 both NGOS, to propagate civil liberties.

Indira Gandhi was detected of violating electoral laws by the Allahabad High Court. Narayan called for Indira to resign and the police to disregard unconstitutional and immortal orders. He started a programme of social transformation which he termed as Sampoorna Kraanti "total revolution". When Gandhi proclaimed a national Emergency on the midnight of 25 June 1975, Narayan, along with opposition leaders were arrested that day. Jayaprakash made a gathering of 100,000 people at the Ramlila grounds and thunderously recited Rashtrakavi Ramdhari Singh 'Dinkar's' wonderfully evocative poetry: *Singhasan Khaali Karo Ke Janata Aaati Hai*. He was detained at Chandigarh even when he asked for one month release to give relief in flooded parts of Bihar. Because of deterioration of his health he was released on 12th November. On account of kidney failure he was on dialysis for the rest of his life.

In the UK, Surur Hoda (a trade unionist who spread the message of Mahatma Gandhi) launched the "Free JP" campaign chaired by Nobel Peace Prize winner Noel Baker for the release of Jayaprakash Narayan. Indira Gandhi revoked the emergency on 18 January, 1977 and announced elections. The Janata Party a vehicle for the opposition to Indira Gandhi, was formed under JP's guidance. The Janata Party was voted into power and became the first non-Congress party to form a government at the Centre. On the call of Narayan, many youngsters joined the JP movement.

Narayan's death occurred in Patna, Bihar on 8 October, 1979, three days before his 77th birthday, due to the effects of diabetes and heart ailments.

Jayaprakash Narayan was remembered specially for leading the mid-1970s opposition against Prime Minister, Indira Gandhi, for whose overthrow he reckoned as total revolution. His biography *Jayaprakash*, was written by his nationalist friend and an eminent writer of Hindi literature Ramavriksha Benipuri. In 1999, he was posthumously awarded the Bharat Ratna, India's highest civilian award, to recognise his social service. Other awards include the Magsaysay award for public service in 1965. The Patna airport is also named after him. The largest hospital run by the Delhi government and the teaching hospital of the famous Maulana Azad Medical College, Lok Nayak Jayaprakash Hospital are also named after him. There is also a park in his name, situated on Bahadur Shah Zafar Marg, in New Delhi, opposite to Maulana Azad Medical College. Jayaprakash Narayan's unflinching love and devotion for his own country made him a great figure in the history of India.

Chapter IV

Swami Sahajanand Saraswati

Swami Sahajanand Saraswati (1889 - 1950) though was born in United Province (present day Uttar Pradesh) was specially remembered for his social and political activities, focussed mostly on Bihar in the initial days and gradually spread to the rest of India with the formation of the All India Kisan Sabha.

Sahajanand Saraswati was born in Deva, Dullahpur, Ghazipur, district in eastern United Province in 1889 to a family of the Bhumihar clan. He was the last of six sons and was then called Naurang Rai. His mother died when he was a child and he was brought up by his aunt. His father 'Beni Rai, was a cultivator and knew little about religion.

The Kisan Sabha movement started in Bihar under the leadership of Saraswati who had formed in 1929 the Bihar Provincial Kisan Sabha in order to support peasant grievances against the zamindari attacks on their rights, and thus encouraging the farmers' movement in India. Gradually the peasant movement intensified and spread across the rest of India. All these radical changes on the peasant front reached its peak point in the formation of the All India Kisan Sabha at the Lucknow session of the Indian National Congress in April 1936 with Saraswati elected as its first President which included prominent leaders like N.G. Ranga and E.M.S. Namboodiripad. The Kisan Manifesto, relased in August 1936, demanded abolition of the zamindari system and cancellation of rural debts. In October 1937, All India Kisan Sabha adopted the red flag as its banner. Soon its leaders became increasingly distant with Congress. After the news of Saraswati's arrest during the Quit India Movement. Subhas Chandra Bose and All India Forward Block decided to observe the 28 of April as All India-Swami Sahajananda Day as a sort of protest.

Saraswati's publications include : *Bhumihar Brahmin Parichay*, in Hindi. *Jhootha Bhay Mithya Abhiman*, in Hindi, *Brahman Samaj Ki Sthiti* in Hindi, *Karmakalap* in Sanskrit and Hindi, etc.

His autobiographical works are :

1. Mera Jeewan Sangharsha (My Life Struggle) in Hindi, *2. Kisan Sabha Ke Sansmaran* (Recollection of the Kishan Sabha) in Hindi, 3. *Maharudra Ka Mahatandav* in Hindi, *4. Jang aur Rashtriya Azadi, 5. Samyukta Kisan Sabha, Samyukta Samajvadi Sabha Ke Dastavez*, etc.

His works related to peasantry and zamindars are :

1. Kisan Kya Karen? 2. Zamindaron Ka Khatma Kaise Ho? 3. Kisan Ke Dost Aur Dushman, 4. Bihar Prantiya Kisansabha Ka Ghoshna Patra, 5. Kisanon Ki Phasane Ki taiyariyan, 6. Rent Reduction in Bihar, How it Works? 7. Zamindari Kyon Utha Di Jaye? 8. Khet Mazdoor (Agricultural Labourer) in Hindi, written in Hazaribagh Central Jail, *9. Jharkhand Ke Kisan, 10. Kisan sabha ke dastavez, 11. Kisan sevak, etc.*

His works translated into English are :

(1) *Swami Sahajanand and the Peasants of Jharkhand ; A view from 1941,* translated and edited by Walter Hauser along with unedited Hindi original (Manohor Publishers, paper back 2005) ;

(2) *Sahajananda on Agricultural Labour and the Rural Poor,* translated and edited by Walter Hauser, Manohar Publishers, paper back 2005 ;

(3) *Religion, Politics and the Peasants*: **A Memoir of India's Freedom Movement**, translated and edited by Walter Hauser, Manohar Publishers, 2003.

His Biographics include :

1. Nilanshu Ranjan, Swami Sahajanand Saraswati, National Book Trust, New Delhi.

2. Raghav Sharan Sharma, Swami Sahajanand Saraswaati, Publications Division, Government of India, 2008.

The official recognition gained by him was that the Government of India issued a commemorative stamp in commemoration of Saraswati on 26 June 2000 by Ram Vilas Paswan, the then Minister of Communications. The Indian Council of Agricultural Research gave the Swamy Sahajanand Saraswati Extension Scientist / Worker Award. In 2001, a two-day Kisan Mahapanchayat was organised on the occasion of the 112th birth anniversarry of Saraswati.

Bihar Governor R.S. Gavai released a book on the life of Saraswati on his 57th death anniversary in Patna.

Saraswati died on 26 June 1950. Subhas Chandra Bose, the leader of the Forward Block commented that Swami Sahajanand Saraswati was in India a name worthmentioning. He was recognised as the undisputed leader of the peasant movement in India, being the idol of the masses and the hero of the millions. Subhas Bose further added that to get him as the chairman of the Reception Committee of the All India Anti-compromise Conference at Ramgarh, was indeed a blessing for all ; further the Forward Block should regard it as a privilege and an honour to obtain him as one of the foremost leaders of the Left movement and as a friend, guide and philosopher of the Forward Block itself. In fact Swami Sahajanand Saraswati took the lead to guide a large number of front rank leaders of the peasant movement having an intimate association with the Forward Block.

Chapter V

B. P. Mondal

Bindheshwari Prasad Mondal (1918-1982) was an Indian Parliamentarian who served as the chairman of the Second Backward Classes Commission (popularly known as the Mondal Commission). B.P. Mondal was a big landlord from Saharsa in Northern Bihar and was a Yadav by caste. The commission's report supported a part of the Indian population known as "Other Backward Classes" (OBCs) and initiated a fierce debate on the policy for under represented and under privileged groups in the Indian politics.

B.P. Mondal came from a community designated as an Other Backward Classes (OBC) in India's system, promoting positive discrimination. Mondal and his wife, Sita Mondal, were survived by five sons and two daughters. The third son, Maninder Kumar Mondal, (popularly known as 'Om Jee') and his son Nikhil Mondal are active in national and state politics. B.P. Mondal died on April 13, 1982. The Government of India issued a stamp in honour of Mondal in 2001. A college named in his honour. B.P. Mondal Engineering College, was founded in 2007.

Mondal was a member of Parliament in Lok Sabha for the State of Bihar from 1967 to 1970 and 1977 to 1979. He was the first OBC Chief Minister of Bihar, governing for 48 days in 1968, a period of intense political instability. In December 1978, Prime Minister Morarji Desai appointed a five member Civil Rights Commission under the Chairmanship of Mondal. The Commission's report was completed in 1980 and recommended that a significant proportion of all government and educational places be reserved for applicants from the Other Backward Classes. The commission report was tabled indefinitely by Prime Minister Indira Gandhi. A decade later, Prime Minister V.P. Singh implemented the recommendations of the Mondal Report.

Chapter VI
Mahapandit Rahul Sankrityayan

Mahapandit Rahul Sankrityayan (9 April 1893 - 14 April 1963), who is called the Father of Hindi Travel Literature was one of the most widely travelled scholars of India, spending fortyfive years of his life on travels away from his home. He was born as Kedarnath Pandey on 9 April 1893 in Azamgarh district in Eastern Uttar Pradesh. His father, Govardhan Pandey, was a farmer from the village Kanaila of Azamgarh district in Uttar Pradesh. His mother, Kulawanti, often stayed with her parents in the village of Kanaila and this is where he was born. He was the eldest of four brothers. He spent part of his childhood in Uttar Pradesh and Bihar. As both parents died when he was still quite young, he was brought up by his grandmother. At the age of nine, he ran away from home to see the world but later returned to his homeland. He received formal schooling at a local primary school, though he later studied and mastered many languages independently, as well as the art of photography.

He travelled different parts of India and throughout the world including Ladakh, Kinnaur and Kashmir. He also travelled many countries like Nepal, Tibet, Srilanka, Iran, China and the former Soviet Union. He spent several years in the "Parsa Gadh" village in the Saran District in Bihar. The village's entry gate is named 'Rahul Gate'. While travelling he secretly went to certain countries. He entered

Tibet as a Buddhist monk. He made several trips to Tibet and brought valuable paintings and Pali and Sanskrit manuscript back to India. Most of these were preserved in the libraries of Vikramshila and Nalanda Universites. In fact, these objects had been taken to Tibet by Buddhist monks during the twelfth and subsequent centuries when Muslim armies had destroyed universities in India. According to some accounts Rahul Sankrityayan employed twenty-two mules to bring these materials from Tibet to India. Patna Museum has a special section of these materials where a number of these are displayed.

Sankrityayan was regarded as a multilingual linguist, proficient in several languages and dialects, including Hindi, Pali, Bhoj puri, Urdu, Persian, Arabic, Tamil, French, Russian etc. He was also a Marxist theoretician, a creative writer. He started writing during his twenties and his works covered a variety of subjects, like Sociology, History, Philosophy, Grammar, Forlklore, Science Drama, and Politics though many of these remained unpublished. One of his most famous books in Hindi is *Volga Se Ganga* (A journey from the Volga to the Ganges) — a work of historical fiction, dealing with the migration of Aryans from the steppes of the Eurasia to regions around the Volga river ; then their movements across the Hindukush and the Himalayas and the subsequent Himalayan regions ; and also their spread to the Indo-Gangetic plains of the subcontinent of India, . The book begins in 6000 BC and ends in 1942, the year when Mahatma Gandhi, the Indian nationalist leader gave a call for Quit India Movement. The Kannada translation was done by B.N. Sharma as "Volga Ganga". The Telugu translation *(Volga Nunchi Ganga Ku)* inspired many readers. *Volga Muthal Ganga Vare,* the Malayalam translation, became greatly popular among the young intellectuals of Kerala and it continues to be one of the most inlfuential books of its times. The Bengali version is *Volga Theke Ganga* which is still praised by the critics.

His works in Hindi are *i.e.* novels :

• *Beesween Sadi* - 1923 ; • *Jeeney ke Liye* - 1940 ; • *Simha Senapathi* - 1944 ; • *Jai Yaudheya* - 1944 ; • *Bhaga Nahin, Duniya ko Badlo* - 1944 ; • *Madhur Swapna* = 1949 ; • *Rajasthani Ranivas* - 1953 ; • *Divodas* - 1960, etc.

Short Stories :

• *Satmi ke Bachche* - 1935 ; • *Volga Se Ganga* - 1944 ; • *Bahurangi Madhupuri* - 1953 ; • *Kanaila Ki Katha* - 1955 - 56.

Autobiography :

• *Meri Jivan Yatra -I* - 1944 ; • *Meri Jivan Yatra - II* - 1950 : • *Meri Jiban Yatra III, IV, V* - Published posthumously.

Biography :

• *Sardar Prithvi Singh* - 1955 ; • *Naye Bharat Ke Naye Neta* (2 volumes) - 1942 ; • *Bachpan Ki Smritiyan* - 1953 ; • *Ateet Se Vartaman (Vol I)* - 1953 ; • *Stalin* - 1954 ; • *Lenin* - 1954; • *Karl Marx* - 1954 ; • *Mao-Tse-Tung* - 1954 ; • *Kaptan Lal* - 1961 ; • *Mahamanav Buddha* - 1956, etc.

Some other books are :

• *Mansik Gulami ;* • *Rhigvedic Arya ;* • *Darshan Digdarshan ;* • *Puratatv Nibandhawali ;* • *Manava Samaj,* • *Madhya Asia Ka Itihas,* etc.

In Bhajpuri :

• *Teen Natak* - 1942 ; • *Panch Natak* - 1942.

In Nepali (Translation) :

• *Bauddhadharnma Darshan* - 1984 ; • *Tibbati Bal - Siksha* - 1933 ; • *Pathavali* (Vol 1, 2, 3) - 1933 ; • *Tibbati Vyakaran* (Tibetan Grammar) - 1933 ; • *Himalaya Parichay Bhag - I ;* • *Himalaya Parichay Bhag - II,* etc.

More than ten of his books have been translated and published in Bengali. Mahapandit was awarded the Padmabhushan in 1963. He received the Sahitya Akademi award in 1958 for his book Madhya Asia Ka Itihaas.

He maintained daily diaries in Sanskrit which were used fully while writing his autobiography. In spite of being a scholar, he wrote in simple Hindi that a common person could follow. He wrote books of varied interests. Being aware of the limitation of Hindi literature, his contribution to make up the loss was in no small measure.

He became a Buddhist monk and took up Marxist Socialism. Sankrityayan was an Indian nationalist, being arrested and jailed for three years for creating anti British writings and speeches. He being referred to as the greatest scholar for his scholarship, was having both proficiency in mathematics and in tackling several language.

The historian Kashi Prasad Jayaswal compared Rahul Sankrityayan with Buddha. Rahul's personality was as impressive and memorable as his achivements. He travelled far and wide and wrote in five languages — Hindi, Sanskrit, Bhojpuri, Pali and Tibetan. His published works cover a wide range including autobiography, biography, travelogue, sociology, history, philosophy, Buddhism, grammar, forlklore, science, fiction drama, essays, politics and pamphleteering Rahulji's Museum Picture Gallery was at his birth place Pandaha. Though he had a little formal education, because of his vast knowledge and command over his subject, University of Leningrad appointed him Professor of Indology in 1937-38 and again in 1947-48.

Chapter VII
Ramdhari Singh (Dinkar)

Ramdhari Singh (Dinkar) (September 23, 1908 - April 24 1974) was an Indian Hindi poet, essayist, patriot and academic. He is regarded as the most important modern Hindi poet. He was also considered to be a poet of rebellion because of his nationalist poetry, written before Indian independence. His poetry dealt with *veer rasa*, and because of his inspiring patriotic compositions, he has been hailed as a national poet. He was also attached to Kavi Sammelan where he wrote regularly.

He was born on September 23, 1908, in Simariya village of Munger district (now in Begusarai district) in Bihar. His father was Babu Ravi Singh and mother was Monroop Devi. During his student life, his favourite subjects were history, politics and philosophy. He studied also Hindi, Sanskrit, Maithili, Bengali, Urdu and English literature. Dinkar was greatly influenced by Tagore, Keats and Milton. He translated the works of Tagore from Bengali to Hindi. The poetic personality of the poet Dinkar was moulded by the pressures and counter-pressures of life during the fredom movement. During his student life in Mokama High School it was not possible for him to stay back during the full school hours as he had to catch the steamer back home. His financial condition was so bad that he couldn't afford to be in the hostel. His poetry touched upon poverty as he himself grew up in such environment. Still he became a nationalist poet. In 1920, Dinker met Mahatma Gandhi for the first time. At this time, in the third decade of the 20th century he founded Manoranjan Library at Simariya. He also edited a hand-written pamphlet.

During his adolescent period, the freedom movement had begun under the leadership of Mahatma Gandhi. In 1929, the movement became yet more aggressive when after matriculation, he entered into Patna College in the intermediate class. Demonstrations were also held in Patna. There was a great rally at Gandhi Maidan in which Dinkerji also participated. During the protest against Simon Commission, the police of the British Government mercilessly lathi charged Lala Lajpat Rai of Punjab; who was severely injured and died. There was a great animation throughout the country. The young Dinker was greatly influenced by such agitations — which inspired him to write poetry.

When a paper called *Chhatra Sahodar* (Brother of students) was published under the editorship of Narsingh Das, Dinker's first poem was published in 1924 or 1925. When in 1928 the peasants' Satyagraha under the leader-ship of Sarder Vallabhbhai Patel was a great success in Bardoli of Gujrat, Dinker wrote ten poems on such basis which was published in a book form under the title *Vijay-Sandesh* (Message of Victory) which is available at present. To avoid the wrath of the Government, Dinker got his poems published under the pscudonym "Amitabh". In 1930, he composed a poem named *Pran-Bhang* (The Breach of Vow), so his poetic career started with *Vijay-Sandes* though before that his poems became a prominent feature of the magazine *Desh*, published from Patna and of *Pratibha*, published from Kannauj. His first collection of poems *Renuka* was published in November 1935.*

He was very much loved by the well-known historian Dr. Kashi Prasad Jaiswal and during the initiative stage of his poetic career he rendered a great help to him in every possible way. He was terribly shocked by his death on

* A copy of which was given to Mahatma Gandhi.

August 4, 1937. Later on he wrote a magazine named *Kalpana* published from Hyderabad "It was good thing that Jaiswalji was my first admirer .... As I heard the news of his death, the world became a dark place for me. I did not know what to do." The historical sense in the poetry of Dinker was first appreciated by Jaiswalji. His work *Urvashi* is apart from other works which mostly deal with *"Veer Rasa"* or the *"brave mode"*. Some of his famous works are *Rashmirathi* and *Parashuram Ki Prateeksha.*

He is regarded as the greatest Hindi poet of *Veer Rasa*. Hindi writer Rajendra Yadev in his novel *Sara Akash* has commented on him that it was really inspiring to read his poetry. Through his poetry, he added, he often probe into Hindu mythology and often made reference to such epical character like Karna. The theme of *Urbashi* deals with the spiritual love of men and women which is quite different from their earthly connection. His *Kurukshetra,* a narrative poem based on *Sanṭi Parva* of the *Mahabharata* ; was composed during the period when the memories of Second World War were fresh in the mind of the poet. Regarding *Karukshetra.* Loknayak Jayaprakash Narayan wrote : "The poetry in Karukshetra centres round the story of *Mahabharata* but in its expression, the soul of today's India seems to reverberate." Acharya Hazeri Prasad Dwivedi wrote : "Such fierce competition between the flow of language and the depth of thoughts, as in *Kurukshetra,* is rarely found. *Kurukshetra* is the pride of our language." His major poetic works are : *Vijay-Sandesh* (1928) (first published), *Pranbhang* (1929) *Renuka* (1935), *Rasavanti* (1939), *Dhoop Chhah* (1946), *Baapu* (1947), *Rashmirathi* (1952), *Neem Ke Patte* (1954), *Neel Kusum* (1954), *Urbashi* (1961), *Parashuram Ki Pratiksha* (1963), *Mritti Tilak* (1964), etc.

Anthologies : Like Lokpriya Kavi Dinker (1960), *Dinker Ki Suktiyan* (1964), *Dinker Ke Geet* (1973), *Sanchoyita* (1973), *Rashmilok* (1974), etc.

Major prose works are like : *Mitti Ki Or* (1946), *Ardhananrishwar* (1952), *Reti Ki Phool* (1954), *Bhaarat Ki Saanskritik Kahaani* (1955), *Ujli Aug* (1956), *Sanskriti Ke Cheer Adhyaay* (1956), *Venu Van* (1958), *Aadhunik Bodh* (1973), *Bhaaratiya Ekta* (1971).

Literary criticism : Like *Sahitya aur Samaj, Lokbharti Prakashan,* New Delhi, 2008, *Chintan Ke Aayam, Lokbharti Prakashan,* New Delhi, 2008, *Kavi aur Kavita,* Lokbharti Prakashan, New Delhi, 2008, etc.

Biographics : Like *Sri Aurobindo : Meri Dristi Mein, Lokbharti Prakashan,* New Delhi, 2008, *Pandit Nehru aur anya mahapurash, Lokbharti Prakashan,* New Delhi 2008, etc.

Translations : Like *Meghduta,* translated by Ramdhari Singh Dinkar.

Rabindranath Ki Kavitanyen (101 selected poems of Tagore) translated by Ramdhari Singh Dinkar along with some others etc.

The Present Prime Minister of India, Narenda Modi wrote a message appreciating the translation of **Rashmirathi** by Dinker into English by the cultural activist Leela Gujadhur Sarup. On 23 November 2012, the President of India, Pranab Mukherjee, gave away Rashtrakavi Ramdhari Singh "Dinkar" Sahitya Ratna Samman. On the occasion, the President recalled the contribution of Ramdhari Singh "Dinkar" in the freedom struggle and his service to Hindi Literature. The poet and former Prime Minister of India Atal Bihari Vajpayee spoke of Dinkerji showing his high respect for him.

Dinkar initially supported the revolutionary movement during the Indian independence struggle, but later on turned into Gandhian. In his *Karukshetra* he accepted the fact that the war is destructive but at the same time commented that it is necessary for the protection of freedom as he was close to prominent nationalists of the time such as Rajendra Prasad, Anugrah Narayan Sinha, Braj Kishore Prasad etc. Being elected three times for Rajya Sabha, he was the member of the house from April 3, 1952 to January 26, 1964. He was awarded the Padma Bhushan in 1959.

Chapter VIII
Phanishwar Nath "Renu"

Phanishwar Nath "Renu" (March 4, 1921 - April 11, 1977) was the most successful writer of the modern Hindi literature in the post-Premchand era, also the author of *Maila Anchal*, which after Premchand's *Godaan*, being regarded as the most significant Hindi novel.

Phaniswar Nath 'Renu' was born on March 4. 1921, at village Aurahi Hingna near Forbesganj, in Araria district (then Purnea district) Bihar. He was educated in India and Nepal. He got primary education in Araria and Forbesganj. He passed his Matriculation from Biratnagar Adarsh Vidyalaya (school) Biratnagar, Nepal. Having passed I.A. from Kashi Hindu Vishvavidyalay (university) in 1942, he participated in the Indian freedom struggle. Gradually he took part in the Nepali revolutionary movement in 1950, resulting in the establishment of democracy in Nepal. He introduced "Anchalik—Katha" (Regional story) of Hindi writing. He was closely associated with Sachehidananda Hirananda Vatsyayana Agyey—his contemporary poet.

The intimacy in writing of Phanishwar Nath brought to the reader with use of local flavour of Hindi was totally a new literary experience. His first novel considered to be his masterpiece *Maila Anchal* (The Soiled Linen 1954) being a social novel narrated the life of rural Bihar and its people, especially the backward and the deprived. He was as a result awarded one of India's highest civilian honours the Padma Sri in 1970, though he returned the award in protest against the proclamation of Internal Emergency. His short story Panchlight (Petromax) has its beauty in its depiction of human bahaviour. There is a great deal of similarity between his and Premchand's writing. Even Katihar railway station has its important place in many of his writings. He also wrote prose which is full of description and rapid character-sketches. He reflected his characters from his own perspective view-point. *Ek Aadim Ratri Ki Mehak* is a straight forward story having a touchy ending. In such story, he deals with the exploration of the emotions of his characters.

His literary works are :

Novels :

• Maila Anchal, • Parti Parikatha, • Juloos &. Janaja • Deerghtapa, • Kitna Chaurahe, • Paltu Babu Road.

Memoirs :

• Rindjal Dhanjal, • Van Tulsi ki gandh, • Shrut Ashrut Purva, • Totapur.

Phanishwar Nath 'Renu' can be regarded as one of the pioneers for expressing the voice of the contemporary rural India through the genre of 'Aanchalik Upanyas' (Regional story) and is considered to be as one of the most well-known Hindi writers who brought regional voices into the mainstream of Hindi literature. His short story *Maare Gaye Gulfam* was adapted into a film *Teesri Kasam* (the Third Vow) by Basu Bhattacharya (produced by the poet-lyricist Shailendra) in 1966 for which he also wrote the dialogues. Later his short story *Panchlight* (Petromax) was made into a TV short film.

Chapter IX
Maghfoor Ahmad Ajazi

Maghfoor Ahmad Ajazi (1900 - 1966) was a well known political leader of Bihar.

Ajazi was born in village Dihuli Block Sakra of District Mazaffarpur, in Bihar on March 3, 1900. His father Moulvi Hafizuddin Husain and grandfather Haji Imam Bakhsh were zamindars and his mother was Mahfoozunnisa. His maternal grandfather Reysat Husain was a reputed advocate of Siamarhi. Ajazi first of all joined Madarsa-e-Imdadia, Darbhanga for religious teachings, then North Brooke Zila School, Darbanga : from there he was expelled for opposing the Rowlatt Act. He passed the matriculation examination from Pusa High School and got admission in B.N. College, Patna for higher studies. He was married to Azizul Fatima, being the daughter of his maternal uncle Moulvi Abul Qasim. He was the disciple of Hazrat Ajaz Husain Budayuni, the Khalif of Hazrat Fazle Rahman Ganj Muradabadi and got the title of 'Ajazi'. 'Ajazi learned the first lesson of patriotism from his father, being a very generous and popular zamindar on one hand and anti-British on other hand. He always protected his subjects from the torture of the Britishers. Once Nilha Saheb of nearby "Bela Kothi" came to give some lesson to Ajazi's father on the basis of misleading information but Saheb was forced to flee away, following the wrath of Hafizuddin's subjects who loved him so much. However, the result was that Saheb had to beg pardon from his father and the conspirator was also punished by the so called saheb. But Hafizuddin pardoned him and even appointed him as his manager.

Ajazi's mother died in his childhooddays and his father died in Lucknow during medical treatment. His elder brother was a freedom fighter and later on was an M.L.A. His younger brother Maulana Mahfoozul Hasan died bachelor at a very tender age at Patna during treatment and was buried there. He had only one sister Noorun Nisa dying issueless.

Ajazi after leaving his studies unfinished at B.N. College at Patna, followed Mahatma Gandhi and joined the Non-cooperation Movement in 1921. After that he took part in freedom movement including boycott and burning of English dresses and articles, breaking of salt Law, Satyagrah, Bharat Chhoro etc. He organised masses against Britishers by volunteer Corps, Charkha Samiti, etc. He collected fund for freedom struggle with the help of "Muthia". Muthia meant to take out a fist of grain before preparing every meal for increasing the fund of freedom struggle. When he was in charge of North Bihar, he once reached the house of his cousin sister situated in a village. When he asked for 'Muthia' he was refused. Rather his sister recognised him, invited him for a meal. But Ajazi flatly denied not only to have a meal but even a glass of water. When his sister took out muthia then he agreed to take a meal, which really shows that he was a man of principle. He boycutted English clothing and articles by burning his own English dresses. He established 'Sewa Dal' organised by Sarajini Naidu and formed 'Ajazi Troop' for training of youngones for freedom movement.

He for the first time met Mahatma Gandhi at Sabarmati Ashram. He also joined Khilafat movement and became a member of Central Khilafat Committee. So he came in contact of Ali brothers *i.e.* Maulana Mahammad Ali Jauhar and Maulana Shaukat Ali and became their close associate. As directed by Md. Ali Jauhar, he took the charge of Khilafat Committee, Kolkata. There he was arrested in a protest march led by Netaji Subhas and was arrested and released at a further most place from Kolkata.

He obtained degree from Kolkata Homoeopathic Medical College. At the time of by-election of Prof. Abdul Bari he was arrested and externed from Purnia district. In August 1942 movement, his house was searched and he worked underground. After the devastating earth quake of 1934, he along with Rajendra Prasad engaged himself in relief operation. Even one night both of them had to sleep beneath a tree, putting their heads on a single brick. Ajazi also was against Jinnah's Two nation theory and the creation of Pakistan. He also founded the All India Jamhur Muslim League to counter Jinnah's All India Muslim League and was its first general secretary. Azazi had to face the wrath of workers of Jinnah's Muslim league for opposing division of Motherland and to create seperate Pakistan. Dr Ajazi being a poet and writer in Urdu language was also an orator. His papers, diaries, letters and files are preserved in the Nehru Memorial Museum and library in New Delhi, National Archives in New Delhi etc.

After independence, Ajazi dedicated his whole life for the well being of the oppressed and for the development of Urdu language. He had got association with trade union movement. He was the president of many important labour unions of North Bihar. He was regarded as a good sportsman and a great lover of sports. He organised many types of sports events and also rural sports in which bull carts race could be regarded as a centre of attraction.

Ajazi played a leading role in Urdu movement in Bihar from the very beginning. He was elected Vice-president of Anjuman Taraqqui-e-Urdu Bihar in 1936. He was the chairman of historic Urdu conference of Muzaffarpur held in 1960, in which for the first time resolution was passed demanding status of second official language for Urdu in Bihar (after fifteen years the demand became reality). Ajazi was behind in power politics after independence. He was nominated by Congress party as an official candidate from Patepur Assembly Constituency (then in Muzaffarpur district of Bihar)., in 1957 general election and his elder brother Manzoor Ahsan Ajazi who then recently rejoined Congress was made a dummy candidate from the same Constituency. With due respect to his brother, he withdrew his candidature and made campaign for his elder brother who won the seat. He got important position in Swatantra Party at State as well as Central level. On direction of Party High Command he contested but unsuccessfully in 1962 Loksabha General Election from Muzaffarpur Parliamentary constituency. Initially everything went on his favour but when Congress candidate Digvijay Narayan Singh realisd his position, he requested the then Prime Minster Jawaharlal Nehru to visit his constituancy. When Nehru visited Muzaffarpur and addressed a huge public gathering at Chakkar Maidan of Muzaffarpur, saying, “Swatantra Party is swearing Muslims on Quran to vote for his canditate”, then his version turned the wave and Ajazi lost. Ajazi died on September 26 at his residence ‘Ajazi house’ in Muzaffarpur city. The road leading to his residence was named ‘Dr Ajazi Marg’ by Muzaffarpur Municipal board in his honour. The famous journalist and the poet Wafa Malikpuri described him an old ‘Mujahid’ (crusader) for Urdu language.

Chapter X
Ram Sharan Sharma

Ram Sharan Sharma (26 November, 1919 - 20 August, 2011) well known an R.S. Sharma, was a famous historian and an academic of ancient and medieval India. Having taught at Patna and Delhi University, he was the visiting faculty at University of Torento. He was a University Grants Commission National Fellow (1958-81) and the President of Indian History Congress in 1975. During his service as the Dean of Delhi University's History Department the major expansion of the department took place in the 1970's. The creations of most of the positions in the Department were the results of his efforts. He was the founding chairman of the Indian Council of Historical Research and a historian of international repute.

Sharma was born in Barauni, Begusarai, Bihar. His father gave him educational support till matriculation. But even after that he got scholarships and did private tutions to carry on his education. In his youth he drew inspiration from Sahajanand Saraswati and scholars like Rahul Sankrityayan to protest against social injustice and the torture of the downtrodden. His association with Dr. Sachchidananda Sinha a social reformer strengthened his ties with the left movement. He was one of the Indian intellectuals who believed that history not only deals with the past but it has also some interconnections with the present.

After passing Matriculation, he joined Patna College, having studied six years from intermediate to post graduate classes. He did his Ph.D. from the School of Oriental and African Studies under the University of London. After having taught at some colleges he came to Patna University for teaching and became the head of the Department of History and a university professor in 1958.

Sharma got the Campbell Memorial Gold medal for 1983 by the Asiatic Society of Bombay in November 1987. He also received K.P. Jayaswal Fellowship of K.P. Jayaswal Research Institute Patna and also received several prizes for his contribution to Indian history. He also got D.Litt from the University of Burdwan. His works have been translated into many Indian languges apart from being written in Hindi and English. Many of his works have been translated into many foreign languages.

Professor Sharma was a great builder of institutions. Because of his supervision the syllabi of the Department of History, Patna University, under went a radical change. He took the initiative of making certain programmes which added a distinct character to the History department of Patna University. Even in Delhi University his contributions are no less significant. He changed the department of history by converting it into secular and scientific approach to History. It is because of his efforts, that the Indian History Congress of which he was the general president in 1975 giving him the honour with H.K. Barpujari Award in 1989, has become the symbol of scientific approach to History.

In his writings Professor Sharma has highlighted on early Indian social stucture, material and economic life, political ideas and the social context of religious ideologies and has sought to underline the historical processes which gave shape to Indian culture and civilisation. Regarding his personality, in the opinion of his student historian

Dwijendra Narayan Jha, "A man of courage, conviction, utter humility and a strong social commitment. Full of compassion he has been a constant source of inspiration to his pupils and other younger Scholars." (Jha, D.N. *Society and Ideology in India*: Essays in Honour of Prof. R.S. Sharma.)

His major works are :

- **Aspects of Political Ideas and Institutions in Ancient India.**
- **Sudras in Ancient India: A Social History of the Lower Order Down to Circa AD 600.**
- **Indias Ancient Past.**
- **Looking for the Aryans.**
- **Indian Feudalism.**
- **Urban Decay in India** etc.

In contrast to his predecessors who had focussed their attention on the study of higher orders, he published his *Sudras in Ancient India* as early in 1958, and examined the relationship of the lower social orders with the means of production from Vedic age up to the Gupta period. In the following year his *Aspects of Political Ideas* and *Institutions in Ancient India*, give emphasis on the material basis of the power structure in Ancient India. In 1965, his *Indian Feudalism* dealt with a major problem whether India passed through the phase of Feudalism: (A system in which people are given law and protection by the lord and work and fight for the lord in return.) His *Urban Decay in India* drew attention to the masses to show the decline of urban centres in early medieval period. In fact his *Indian Feudalism* in 1965 brought about a great deal of animation in the academic world. The work has been the centre of attraction. His books on *Looking for the Aryans* and *Advent of the Aryans in India* demolished the myth that the Aryans were the original people of India and Harappa culture their creation.

His 1977 *Ancient India* was banned by the Janata Party Government in 1978, among other things for its criticism of the historical role of Krishna and the events of the Mahabharata epic. He has supported the addition of the Ayodhya dispute and the 2002 Gujarat riots to the school syllabus to widen the mental horizons of youngstars.

After his death, at a function organised by the Indian Council of Historical Research, eminent historians Romila Thapar, Irfan Habib, Satish Chandra and others paid homage to Sharma and highlighted his contributions.

During his life time he was the author of 115 books, written in fifteen languages. He gave major decisions related to historical research in India as the head of the department of History at Patna and Delhi University. His great effort solved the border dispute as recorded by Sachidananda Sinha in a letter to Rajendra Prasad. The fellow historian Professor Irfan Habib opined, "D.D. Kosambi and R.S. Sharma together with Daniel Thorner, brought peasants in the study of Indian history for the first time." (*Essays in Indian History*).

Odisha

Chapter I
Gopabandhu Das

Gopabandhu Das (1877-1928) known as Utkalamani (gem of Odisha) was a social worker as well as a reformer, political activist, journalist, poet and essayist.

Being born on 9th October 1877 near Puri, Odisha. Gopabandhu was a pioneer in the Indian culture. His father was Shree Daitari Das and his mother was Swarnamayee Devi. He when he was twelve years of age, married Apti, but continued his education. After completing primary education he joined Puri Zilla School in 1893 where he met his teacher Mukhtiar Ramchandra Das, who was not only a genius but also a nationalist. In fact the very teacher taught him some values of life. The inadequate response of authorities for the victims of cholera motivated him to start a voluntary corps Puri Seva Samiti ; this movement later led to the establishment of a separate hospital for cholera patients at Puri.

During his youth time, the Oriya literary world was divided between the ancient, *The Indradhanu* and the modernists the *Bijuli*. He believed that a nation as well as its literature survive by their tradition. His satirical poem in *The Indradhanu* led him to be punished by the Inspector of Schools. But he was mentally strong enough not to ask for pardon, rather to accept panishment. He attended Ravenshaw College, Cuttack in spite of his father's death. During this period, he started Kartavya Bodhini Samiti (Duty Awakening society) to inspire his friends to do some social services when they were faced by some social, economic and political problems and also to serve the poor. While studying at Ravenshaw college he himself was commited to do such social service. While suddenly his son got ill, he rushed to the flood-affected areas in the interior area of the district to provide relief to the people. Even when his son died he had no sense of regret. Rather he said, "There are so many to look after my son. What more can I do? But there are so many people crying for help in the affected areas and it is my duty to go there. Lord Jagennath is here to take care of the boy." Even when he got the news of his success in law examination, his wife died.

In Kolkata he started a labour union and night schools for Oriya labourers. His association with Vande Mataram group inspired to develop in him nationalist spirit. His motto was to reform society by improving educational system. Returning from Kolkata he for a short time worked as a government lawyer in Mayurbhanj Court. But he had no interest for law, therefore he gave up his practice to work for the well-being of the people. With the mission that education can only bring improvement for society, he established his famous Satyabadi Bana Vidyalaya in the year 1909 at Sakshi Gopal, a place of pilgrimage near Puri. In fact the source of his inspiration was Santiniketan, established by Rabindranath, as Gopabandhu being the admirer of the old Gurukul Ashrama system of education. His Bana Vidyalaya was set in the midst of natural surroundings of Bakul and Chhuriana trees as Gopabandhu opined that education means all-around development of a child. As he didn't believe in caste system, so he allowed all children of all castes to study and dine together, so a cordial relationship developed between the teacher and the taught in his school. He also gave emphasis on co-curriculer activities of the children. Gopabandhu wanted to infuse national feelings in students with the help of education and also taught them the value of social service. In this way though Gopabandhu's first assignment in his job was a teacher and though he gave it up to become a lawyer to try his practice at various places, later on he decided too quit his job for social service and mass education. This was well-evident when he established such school like Satayabadi with the same mission in mind. Because of its rising success, it was converted into a National School in the year 1921.

Gopabandhu's political career began with Utkal Sammilani in 1903. At the same time he made persuasion to others to merge with the National Congress to make the Odia movement a part of the Indian National Movement. He had to lead prison life several times for joining in the freedom movement. He left Congress, because of some inner trouble among the leaders aiming for power and dedicated his life in the service of the people. Next he was national Vice president of Lok Sevak Mandal till his death.

He became a member of the Old Bihar and Odisha Legislative Council for four years from 1917 to 1920. He dealt with four major problems (a) blending of all the Odia speaking tracts, (b) permanent steps to be taken for the prevention of floods and faminine in Odisha, (c) restoration of Odia's right to manufacture salt free from excise duty, (d) the system of education be introduced on Satyabadi model. He regularly attended the annual meeting of the Utkal Sammilani, being elected the President in 1919. He was the first leader of Odisha to organise Odisha Provincial Committee. Being the first President of the Congress Party in Odisha, he brought Gandhiji to Odisha in 1921 to pave the path for Non-cooperation Movement. After being arrested he was put to jail for two years in 1922. He was free from Hazaribagh jail on June 26, 1924. Subhas Bose regarded him as the father of the national movement in Odisa. Besides he also took a main part in Press Freedom in Odisha. He gave emphasis specially on language being the foundation of unity. In his opinion oneness of language makes the unity stronger.

He was also the pioneer of Odia Movement, a freedom fighter and a renowned social reformer. He was a famous educationist in the sense that he took the initiative for the establishment of Satyabadi School at Satyabadi in the Puri District. He was responsible for rousing patriotic-sense in the students so that they could give a brave fight against the Britishers. His dedication of life for the service of the people could be aptly placed on his own utterance — "Let my body mingle in the dust of my motherland and let my countrymen walk across it ; and let my flesh and bones fill in the potholes of my country's self independence."

He also played a vital role in making Oriya journalism appropriate for the masses. His publication of a monthly magazine called Satyabadi in 1914, and his weekly newspaper *The Samaja*, the most popular one of which he was the edior till his death, testyfy to such fact. However at the time of attending a ceremony on collecting funds for the flood affected people of Odisha, in Lahore he fell sick, he never recovered, his prolonged illness brought his death on July 17, 1928.

Pundit Gopabondhu Das was really a versatile genius. In spite of being a social reformer, he was also a poet and a writer. Some of his poems like 'Kara Kabita', 'Dharmapada', 'Bandi Ra Atma Katha' really echo his proficiency as a poet. In spite of certain personal set backs like losing his parents in his childhood, also his wife, son and younger, brother in his young age, he never resigned himself to his fate. He completed his educational career and sacrificed his life for the improvement of the miserable condition of the people of Odisha. He can be regarded as the great son of the state. Mahatma Gandhi commented on him that "Gopabandhu was one of the noblest sons of Odisha."

Chapter II
Madhusudan Das

Madhusudan Das (28 April 1848 - 4 February 1934) was born on 28 April 1848 in a village called Satyabhamapur, 20 kilometres from Cuttack, Odisha.

He is famous as Kulabruddha which means Grand Old Name of Utkal Gaurab which means Pride of Utkal and was recognised as a poet and freedom fighter. He was the first graduate and also the first advocate of Odisha. Being born to a Zamindari family his father was Choudhuury Raghunath Das and mother Parbati Debi. He was called by his parents Gobindaballabh at the initial stage but later on he was given the name Madhusudan. He had two elder sisters and a younger brother named Gapalballabh. Madhusadan had adopted two Bengali girls ; Shailabala and Sudhansubala Hazra. Shailabala was a well-known educationist who trained herself from England and after whose name the famous Shailabala Women's College of Cuttack was established, Shailabala being a Bengali, was left by her parents in the care of Madhusudan Das and his wife Saudamini Devi at Kolkata. Sudhansubala Hazra being a Bengali was the first female lawyer of British India. Ashutosh Mukherjee, the former Vice Chancellor of Kolkata University in Kolkata had Madhubabu as his house-tutor and he was also the house teacher of Janakinath Bose, father of Subhash Chandra Bose at Ravenshaw College.

Madhusudan Das started his early education at a village-school. He was well-versed in many subjects and also studied Persian from a Maulavi. After completing his early education, he studied at Cuttack High School (later known as Ravenshaw Collegiate School) which offered English education. In 1864, he passed the Entrance examination and went to Kolkata University. In spite of going through some adverse circumstances, he resided in Kolkata for fifteen years from 1866 to 1881. In 1870, he was the first Odia to complete his B.A., completed M.A. and B.L. degrees. He became the first scholar from Odisha to achieve such merits.

Having returned to Odisha from Kolkata in 1881, he began practising legal cases. Having great knowledge in that field he earned much and could spend it for the common people. He acted as a source of inspiration to the lawyers of Odisha and in India. Even his birth anniversary is observed as Lawyer's Day in the state.

Being called "Madhu Babu" by the common people he devoted his life for the political, social and economic improvement of the people of Odisha and did service for his motherland as a lawyer, social reformer and patriot. He established Utkal Sammilani' which brought a revolution in the industrial and social development of Odisha. By his political struggle, he brought the unification of Odisha and modern Odisha had its birth on 1st April 1936. The very day is celebrated as Utkal Dibasa.

He got also appreciation as a legislator and journalist. He was the first Oriya to be the member of both the legislative council and the Central Legislative Assembly of India.

He was the first Indian Minister and he was also the first Oriya to sail overseas. He was also the founder of Utkal Tannery in 1905, a factory manufacturing shoes and other leather products. In 1897, he established the Orissa Art Ware Works. Because of his cooperation and support, The Tarakasi (filigree) work of silver ornaments, gained its own ground.

As a writer and a poet, a feeling of patriotism was focussed in all his literary works. He wrote a number of articles and poems in English as well as in Odia language. Some of his important poems are 'Utkal Santan', 'Jati Itihash', 'Jananira Ukti' etc. He was also a good orator in Oriya, Bengali and English. He sacrificed his whole life as well as his wealth for the welfare of his country. Mahatma Gandhi regarded him as a great Indian patriot who dedicated wholly his life for some national schemes to have their definite ground and commendable feet.

Chapter III

Krushna Chandra Gajapati

Krushna Chandra Gajapati (26 April 1892 - 25 May 1974) popularly known as Maharaja Sir Krushna Chandra Gajapati Narayana Dev played a major role in forming Independent Odisha State. He is in fact the architect of the modern Odisha state. The present Gajapati District of Odisha was named after him. He was the Honorary Captain in the First World War. He was really interested in Oriya literature, art, music, culture, sports ; specially he showed a great deal of excellence in horse-riding.

Maharaja Krushna Chandra Gajapati Narayan Dev, the younger member of the great Ganga Dynasty of Paralakhemundi, was born on April 26 1892. His father was King of Paralakhemundi Goura Chandra Gajapati and his mother was Radhamani Devi. After receiving his education at the initial stage at the local Maharaja High School he then entered the exclusive Newington College in Madras for higher studies. During his studies in Madras, he lost his father Shri Goura Chandra Gajapati.

After the completion of his studies at Madras he returned to Paralakhemundi and in the year 1913 married the Princess of Kharasuan State. In the the same year he held the reign of this state on April 26, 1913.

Maharaja Krushna Chandra Gajapati had a vital role to play in the Oriya movement for forming an Independent Odisha state on the basis of language and unity of the nation. He spent out much from his royal treasury to materialise the effort. Utkal Gourav Madhusudan Das, Utkalamani Gopa-bandhu Das, Maharaja Krushna Chandra Gajapati and others demanded a separate Odisha state. This proposal was approved in the Bihar-Orissa Legislative Assembly. As a member of the Utkal Sammilani, he proposed a separate Odisha State in the first Round table conference held in London on November 16, 1930. Finally on his own initiative and Utkal Sammalani the separate state of United Odisha was formed on April 1, 1936. Gajapati's own state of Paralakhemundi in Vizagapatam district was divided into two — with the capital and most of the princely states coming under Orissa and the remaining Telugu-majority areas remained in Madras Presidency. In 1937, the first Governor of Odisha, Sir John Austin Hubback invited Krushna Chandra Gajapati Dev to form the cabinet. Krushna Chandra was the first Prime Minister of the Odisha State from April 1, 1937 to July 18, 1937 and was on the same post for the second time from November 24, 1941 to June 30, 1944.

He took a major role in establishing Utkal University, the SCB Medical College and also the famous Central Rice Research Institute of the Bidyadharpur, Cuttack, being the largest of the kind in Asia. He also established many hospitals, schools, colleges, industrial institutions, agricultural farms and supplied a record number of 1281 water tanks in his agriculturally dominated region. For this reason, the undivided Ganjam District was called the rice bowl of Odisha. On his inspiration and guidance, the poor but meritorious students were given scholarships in humanities, science, agriculture, medicine, etc.

Being an Honorary Captain in the First World War, he received a rare Sanod in 1920 from the then Viceroy and Governor General of India, because of his services to the India Army during the Great War as a mark of praise and recognition. He was both the members of the Royal

Commission on Agriculture and also of Madras Legislative Council.

After receiving the award of honorary Doctorates by the Utkal University and Berhampur University, he was appointed a Knight Commander of the Order of the Indian Empire in 1946. He was the founder of Indian Constitution, being a member of the Constituent Assembly of India. His contribution to horse racing and his encouragement for horse breeding in India are remarkable. Though he died on May 25, 1974, at 82, he had many relatives, friends and advisers to appreciate his contribution for his own country. He was given a state funeral by the Government of Odisha and was cremated with full of honours at Paralakhemundi.

Chapter IV
Harekrushna Mahatab

Harekrushna Mahatab (November 21, 1899 - January 2, 1987), being a leader of the Indian National Congress was regarded as a prominent figure in the Indian independence movement. He was popularly famous as Utkal Keshari.

Harekrushna Mahatab took his birth at Agarpada village in Bhadrak district of Odisha. His parents were Krushna Charan Das and Tohapha Devi. Having passed his matriculation examination from Bhadrak High School he joined Ravenshaw College, Cuttack, but left his studies in 1921 to join the independence movement.

Since he encouraged rebellion against the government, he was put to jail. He was the chairman of Balasore District Board from 1924 to 1928. He was also the member of Bihar and Odisha Council in 1924. Having joined the Salt Satyagraha movement, he was imprisoned again in 1930. After being elected as the General Officer Commanding of Congress Sevadal, he was put to arrest when the party was banned. He also took participation in the movement against untouchability in 1934 and made his ancestral temple open for all for first time in Odisha. He was the President of Utkal Pradesh Congress Committee from 1930 to 1931 and again in 1937. He was nominated to the Congress Working Committee by Subhas Chandra Bose in 1938 and continued till 1946 and again from 1946 to 1950. He was also the President of State People's Enquiry Committee in 1938 and recommended that the former princely states should merge with Odisha Province. He joined in the Quit India Movement in 1942 and was in prison from 1942 to 1945.

Mahatab was the first Chief Minister of Odisha from April 23, 1946 to May 12, 1950. He was also the Union Minister of Commerce and Industry from 1950 to 1952. He was the secretary general of the Congress Parliamentary Party in 1952. He was the Governor of Bombay from 1955 to 1956. After giving resignation from Governorship in 1956, he became again the Chief Minister of Odisha from 1956 to 1960. During his period of service as the Chief Minister, he took a great part in merging and integrating former princely states, shifting the capital from Cuttack to Bhubaneshwar and took initiation in contruction of Hirakund Dam Project. He was elected to the Lock Sabha in 1962 and was the Vice President of the Indian National Congress in 1966. But in the same year he resigned from the Congress and led the Orissa Jana Congress. He died in January 2, 1987.

He also founded Prajatantra" Prachar Samiti and started the weekly magazine, "Prajatantra" in 1923 at Balasore which later became the "Daily Prajatantra". He was also the chief editor of a monthly journal Jhanker since its existence. He was awarded the Sahitya Academy award in 1983 for the third volume of his well-known work *Gaon Majlis.* He was the President of Orissa Sahitya Academy and Sangit Natak Academy for some time. He received an honorary Doctorate degree from Aadhra University, an honorary D.Lit from Utkal University and an honoary Doctorate of Law from Sagar University.

Chapter V
Biju Patnaik

Biju Patnaik (March 5, 1916 - April 17, 1997) was an Indian politician and became the Chief Minister of Odisha for two terms.

Biju Patnaik, being born on March 5, 1916 was the child of Lakshminarayan and Ashalata Patanaik. His parents belonged to G. Nuagan Bhanjanagar, Ganjam district around 80 km. from Baramhapur. Though he was educatd at Ravenshaw College in Odisha but he was trained as a pilot because of his interest in aviation. At first he was associated with private airlines but at the beginning of the Second World War he joined the Royal Indian Air Force, ultimately he was the head of air transport command. While in service he became interested in politics.

Biju Patnaik met Jawaharlal Nehru when he participated in Indian freedom struggle becoming his trusted friend. In Nehru's view the freedom struggle for Indonesian people had got some similarity with India's struggle for freedom. When the Dutch tried to subdue Indonesian independence on July 21, 1947, President Sukarno ordered Sjahrir, the former Prime Minister of Indonesia, to leave the country to attend the first Inter Asia Conference, organised by Nehru, July 1947 and to incite public opinion against the Dutch. But Sjahrir couldn't do that as the air routes and the Indonesian sea were controlled by the Dutch. Then Nehru asked Patnaik, who was adventurous and an expert pilot to rescue Sjahrir. Biju Patnaik and his wife flew to Java and brought Saltan Sjahrir reaching India via Singapure on July 24, 1947. For this kind of bravery Patnaik was given honorary citizenship in Indonesia and was given the title "Bhoomi Putra", the highest Indonesian award. At the time of celebration of Indonesia's 50th Independence Day, Patnaik was awarded the highest national award the 'Bintang Jasa Utama'. He also had a role to play in saving Kashmir from enemies and on this issue he was also very loyal for following Nehru's order.

Biju Patnaik piloted the first plane that left Palam airport at Delhi on October 27, 1947 at dawn and landed at Srinagar Airport in the early morning. He was accompanied by 17 soldiers of SIKH regiment, headed by Lt. Col. Dewan Ranjit Rai. He followed the instructions of the Prime Minister Nehru that if the airport was taken over by the enemy then he was not to land. So he at first ensured that none was around and that the air strip was vacant. The raiders actually were busy in the distribution of war booty among themselves in Baramulla.

Patnaik's political ideals were based on socialism and federalism. In 1946, Patnaik was elected uncontested to the Odisha Legislative Assembly from North Cuttack Constituency. In 1961, he assumed the presidency of the State Congress. Under his leadership, the Congress party won 82 of 140 seats and Patnaik (representing Chowdwar Constituency) became the Chief Minister of Odisha on 23 June, 1961 and remained in the position until October 2, 1963. He was the Chief Minister of Odisha at the age of 45.

Patnaik was close to Indira Gandhi who took over the charge of Congress Party in 1967 though they had a clash in 1969 over the Presidential election. However, after leaving Congress, he framed a regional party the Utkal Congress. In the 1971 assembly poll, his party did well. Next he again came in close contact with his friend Jayarprakash Narayan and joined his movement when it was at its peak in 1974. During the time of Emergency in 1975, Biju Patnaik was arrested along with others.

After his release in 1977, in the same year he was elected to the Lok Sabha for the first time from Kendrapara and became Union Minister for steal and mines during the time of Morarji Desai and the Charan Singh Govenment until 1979. He was re-elected to the Lok Sabha again in 1980 and 1984 from Kendrapara as Janata Party Candidate. After the defeat of Congress in 1989, he again came to the forefront. Though he played a main role in helping V.P. Singh to gain the post of the Prime Minister, he preferred to go back to Odisha to be prepared for the assembly election. In 1990, state Assembly Election when the Janata Dal gained a major position by winning two third assembly seats, Biju Patnaik became the Chief Minister of Odisha for the second time until 1995. After his re-election to the Lok Sabha in 1996 from Cuttack and Aska Constituencies as a Janata Dal candidate, he however was capable of retaining the latter till his dealth on April 17, 1997 following cardio-respiratory failure.

His achievements as a public representative, included Kalinga tubes, Kalinga Airlines, Kalinga Iron Work, Kalinga Refractories and "the Kalinga", a daily Oriya Newspaper. He took a great deal of initiative in such projects as the Port of Paradip, Orissa aviation centre, Bhubaneswar airport, the Cuttack-Jagatpur Mahanadi highway bridge, Regional Engineering College, Rourkela, Orissa University of Agriculture and Technology, Bhubaneswar etc. He also established the Kalinga Cup in football.

When the Central Government refused to give funds to build the Paradeep Port, he commented, "to hell with the Government of India, I will build the port with state Government and my own money." Really he spent Rs. 1.60 billion for such project and later on Nehru sanctioned funds for the project. At present Paradeep Port is Odisha's most prominent port. On being criticised in the Parliament for his decision to provide more help to Odisha, Nehru's reply was, "Biju Patnaik has the courage, dynamism and zeal to work. So there is no blunder in giving more aid to Odisha." Even during the Sino-Indian War in 1962, Nehru took advice from the Oriya leader repeatedly. So he was unofficially Nehru's defence advisor for some time.

Patnaik also had to fight against corruption, the social vice, though his government failed to eradicate corruption to a greater part. The Government of Odisha has given names to several institutions after his name, which include, Biju Patnaik Airport at Bhubaneswar, the Biju Patnaik University of Technology, Biju Patnaik Stadium etc. His son Naveen Patnaik made his birthday a holiday in Odisha in his memory. When a journalist asked him on his 79th birthday how he wanted to die, he replied, "I would like to die in an air crash rather than from prolonged illness. I would like to die instantly, just fall down and die."

Biju Patnaik message was for the people Orissa. "To be born poor is not a crime but to remain so is indeed a crime. Be loyal not to me but to the destiny of the State." His hope was, "In my dream of the 21st century for the State, I would have young men and women who put the interest of the State before them. They will have pride in themselves, confidence in themselves. They will not be at anybody's mercy, except their own selves. By their brains, intelligence and capacity they will recapture the history of Kalingo."

Chapter VI
Nabakrushna Choudhury

Nobakrushna Choudhury (born on November 23, 1901 at Cuttack, Odisha, India. died 1984) was an Indian politician and activist. He was the Chief Minister of the Indian State of Odisha. He hailed from a landlord family of Kherasa village of Jagatsinghpur District, Odisha. His father, Gokulananda Choudhury was a great advocate. Naba-krushna revealed unusual talents during his child-hood. He liked games and sports very much. As he was more interested in games and sports, his father appointed a private tutor for him for study. As a result, he was educated at the Peary Mohan Academy and prepared himself for Matriculation Examination at the age of 14. But he had to wait for two years and passed the examination with a good division.

In 1917, Nabakrushna Choudhury was admitted in the Ravenshaw College Cuttack. At about this time, his brother Gopabandu Choudhury resigned from government service to serve the people of Odisha. That year the people of Russia had achieved victory by fighting against the oppressive king which inspired Nabakrushna Choudhuri much. In order to devote himself for the service of his country, he left his college. At that point his father died and his elder brother became his guardian. In 1921 Gandhiji was organising the people for taking up constructive programmes, the most important of which was to attain self sufficiency in clothes through spinning and weaving.

Since spinning and weaving had been completely stopped in Odisha in 1922, Nabkrushna Choudhury went to Sabarmati in Gujrat to learn about Khadi—the principles of spinning and weaving. Gandhiji was living in an Ashram in Sabarmati, within ten months Nabakrushna learnt all about khadi. After his return to Odisha, Nabakrushna tried to introduce Gandhian constructive programme in Odisha in spite of his opposition from his family members. In the same year, he used to teach with his brother Gopabandhu in a new type of school established by his brother at Alakashram, in Odisa. Correlation between head and the hands was the hallmark of Alakashram. He (Nabakrushna) also went to Santiniketan to have his study from Tagore. In course of time, during his stay there, he came in contact with Malati Choudhury (Nee sen) to marry her later.

After their marriage, they, led a very simple life. They went to Tarikund near Jagatsinghpur. There Nabakrushna worked hard on the land, (which belonged to his father). Nabakrushna and his wife jointly produced sugarcane, potato and groundnut. They in this way, totally identified themselves with the people of Tarikund. After the birth of their eldest daughter, Uttara, Nabakrushna gave much attention to the child, along with his wife. However the village people specially the women folk took it badly, though such an example was really a lesson for this whole village-community. In the village besides agriculture both Nabakrushna and Malati Devi wanted to spread literacy and adult education among the illiterate villagers.

In 1920, Lavana Satyagraha started in response to the law of the British to disallow the people to get salt out of sea water in the coastal areas of Gujarat and Odisha. Nabababu gave a lead to the movement for which he was imprisoned for four months. But he in stead of being afraid, spent the time in study and also in planning games and gymnastics for his fellow prisoners. In 1931 Gopabandhu and his family were in prison. All of them were transferred to Hazaribag jail. Nababbu met Minoo Masani, Ashok Mehta, Jayaprakash Narayan and shared with them his ideas on the freedom struggle. After his return to Tarikund from Hazaribag Jail, he formed a small group within Congress and began editing and publishing a journal named 'Sarathi' which was the mouth piece of both farmers and labourers and to carry on the expenditure of the journal, Malati Devi sold her ornaments. Later on Nababbu's small group was merged into the Congress Socialist Party, formed in India with the founders like Ram Monohor Lohia, Acharya Narendra Dev and Jayaprakash Narayan. The purpose of the Navayuga Sahitya Samsad, formed on Nababbu's own initiative, was to create progressive literature in Odisha.

Odisha took its origin as a seperate province on the first of April 1936. In 1937, during the elections of the Odisha Legislative Assembly, held for the first time, Nababbu contested against Raj Bahadur Chintamani Acharya from the Tirtal-Ersama constituency and had an overwhelming majority in the election. His political career began in this way. As an MLA, he took a great deal of interests regarding the poor and the downtrodden people of Odisha when the farmers took a firm stand against the landlords, being oppressed by them, Nabakrushna started another journal named 'Krusak', dealing with the problems of the farmers and labourclass.

Odisha had twentysix princely states, not governmed by the British. The chiefs used to govern their states in their own way by paying a royalty to the British. Though the Congress party followed a policy of non-interference with the princely states Nababbu didn't believe in such policy. Malati Devi, Harmohan Patnaik, Gouranga Charan Das etc. also supported his belief. There was stiff resistance against the princely state of Nilgiri. Dhenkanal was also well-known for its oppression to the people. Nababbu, accompanied by Harmohan Patnaik, the President of Dhenkanal

Praja Mandal, tried to fight against the rulers of the princely states. They visited all the houses of the villages around Dhenkanal, made it clear about the oppressional strategy of the Raja of Dhenkanal. In 1938 he was again jailed for his involvement in the Praja Mandal Movement.

The most significant event of Dhenkanal oppression was the sacrifice of 12 years old Bajiraut who died by the bullets of Dhenkanal forces along with others. Nababbabu and Malati Devi further strengthened the movement. In 1940, Nababbabu was imprisoned for six months as an individual Satyagrahi. On August 8, 1942, Gandhiji gave his call called "Do or Die" which had a great effect on the people. Before August 9, Gandhiji and all the important leaders including Nababbabu were imprisoned. Nababbabu was in Cuttack, Angul and Puri prisons mixing with the fellow prisoners and organising them against the misdeeds of the jail employees. Nababbabu was sent to Berhampur jail from Puri jail. On January 26, 1944, some young prisoners hoisted the National flag in spite of the attacks of the jail and police personnel to resist it. Then by the order of the District British Megistrate the prisoners were beaten up. Then the District Megistrate gave the firing orders. Nababbabu, hearing such orders, appeared to face the gun. The British officers, being afraid of him, withdraw the firing orders. By the end of 1945, Nababbabu was released from the Barhampur jail.

In 1946 elections, Nababbabu won from the north Kendrapara Constituency, becoming a Cabinet Minister in the Indian National Congress Government, having the Revenue, Supplies and Forest Departments under his charge. He was so involved regarding the problems of the people, that he had no time to attend his family. Even his wife engaged herself in working in tribal areas. In 1948, their only son Vinayak born later committed suicide which shocked Nababbabu, as a result, he resigned from the government and decided to work for the people. He was also the organiser of Basic Education for the state of Odisha. He had to put all his labour to make basic education, applicable for real life. In spite of Jawharlal Nehru's (The Prime Minister of India) request to become the Chief Minister of India, he didn't agree to be. Then through the persnasion of Malati Devi he became the Chief Minister.

During Nabababu's regime as the Chief Minister, the ageold Zamindari system was finally abolished. The farmers were no more tortured by the Zamindar and became the owners of the lands. Nababahu's experience as the Revenue Minister was of great help in this respect. He also had a great concern for the welfare of the people. The Hirakud Dam was constructed during Nababahu's Chief Ministership. Many offered resistance and opposition to its construction. However because of Nababahu's determination and firmness, the construction of Dam was possible.

During that time, some officers were unwilling to visit the tribal areas, some officers were torturing the tribal people. The tribals were also exploited by the money-lenders. As a result of such exploitation, the tribals of Koraput District made a revolt against the officers and moneylenders. Though the government officers tried their best to suppress the fact, Nababahu had the spirit enough to send some officers for the well-being of the people. Even he personally visited those areas to know about the problems of the tribal people and to have some sympathy for them, so the government officers, farmers and money-lenders didn't have the courage to exploit them.

Nababahu had the realisation that a people-oriented government had to use Oriya as its language for communication and administration. So he formulated rules for using Oriya in the administrative process. As an MLA Nababahu spoke in Oriya in the Assembly and had discussions in the same language. Then Odisha Legislative Assembly was constituted in 1946, again the question of language to be used in the Assembly was raised. Nabababu's demand that Oriya the peoples' language to be used was accepted and retained. Even Nabababu's decision to use Oriya as the language for communication and administration met strong opposition by senior officers in the administration. But Nabababu didn't pay head to all these ; so Oriya was the language to be used for administration. But all his initiatives were in vain, when he left the government in October 1956. To him to serve the people was more important than power.

Acharya Vinoba Bhave launched the Bhoodan and Gramdan movement when Nababu was the Chief Minister. He took a great initiative in the movement, moving with Vinoba to spread the message of Gramdan. The government help was not at all rendered in any way in this respect. In 1959, Nabababu and Mridula Sarabhai worked hard for Kashmir issue. Many Kashmiri leaders met him at Angul for discussion. In 1959, his journey to Srinagar was for a top level diplomatic mission. He had interaction with top political leaders and military officers.

At that time Nagas were organising themselves to be separated from India. A great deal of violence took place. Even military intervention by Government could not check the Nagas. Through the establishment of an institution called peace centre at Mohakchung, Nabababu and Jayaprakash had a talk with the people to deal with their problems. After Joyprakesh, Nabababu was the Director of the Peace Centre. The Nagas in the mean time stopped their hostile activities.

Today Bangladesh was a part of Pakistan, known as East Pakistan. In the name of religion some persons were torturing the Hindus who were migrating to India. Some of them came to live in Odisha. The Hindus on the other hand took revenge on the Muslims by torturing them. So it had its repercussions in Odisha, specially in Rourkela.

Nababāābu and others went to Rourkela, worked among both the communities till the situation became calm.

Naxalites were quite active in another part of Odisha, *i.e.* Koraput. The poor tribal people were exploited by the rich people. The Naxalites unable to tolerate such oppression started killing the rich. The Government tried to control such anarchy. In the name of law and order, atrocities were committed on the people by the police. Hearing such news, Nababābu and Malati Devi went there to organise meetings at different places to get into the truth of it. Peace workers from different parts of the world came there. Gradually atrocities came to a stop. The Naxalite leader, Nagabhusan Patnaik was put to death for his Naxalite activities. Nababābu inturn wrote to his friend President Sayeeva Reddy for excusing the offence of Nagabhusan. Others Naxalites were also pardoned and released.

In 1974, corruption ruled over everywhere in the country. Those belonging to government service earned a huge amounts of money by unfair means and caused a great deal of suffering to the common people. Jayaprakash Narayan expressed his dissatisfaction to such corruption. He asked the young people to fight against this. As a sort of protest the Prime Minister Mrs. Indira Gandhi declared National Emergency in the country in 1975. During the Emergency Nababābu, Malati Devi and others were imprisoned. Nababābu was sent to Baripada Jail and Malati Devi to Cuttack Jail though Nababābu became sick in Baripada Jail ; he developed partial paralysis. However he was concerned about the problems of common people. Even his family members were very much disturbed and asked him to keep out of politics. But as people were his life, he couldn't but to think about them. When he was released, the doctors put some restrictions on his movements. Malati Devi was also released from Cuttack Jail. Both of them departed to Angul.

The Government of India was subject to criticism throughout the world. Indira Gandhi was forced to withdraw Emergency Rule. The result was another general election in India, The party in power thought that it was the exact time to hold election as may leaders were in jail and also the opposition lacked financial resources. But just the opposite happened. Many important leaders, including Indira Gandhi were defeated miserably. This was the people's mandate. Nababapu was really happy over this.

Nababapu had many bereavements. His grandson and grand nephew died of road accidents. Besides he was really shocked by the selfish atitude of the educated people and the poverty of the common people. By mid June 1984, Nababapu's health deteriorated and when he was 83, he died of massive heart attack.

Chapter VII
Fakir Mohan Senapati

Fakir Mohan Senapati (January 13, 1843 - June 14, 1918) was born in January 13, 1843 at Mallikashpur in Balasore. His father was Laxman Charan Senapati and his mother was Tulsi Devi Senapati. Fakir Mohan devoted his life for the progress of Odia language in the 19th and early 20th century. Vyasa Kabi Fakir Mohan Senapati married Leelavati Devi in the year 1856 when he was only thirteen. When he was twenty nine years, she died. In summer 1871, he again married to Krushna Kumari Devi. His comment about her was that "I seemed as if God had sent me Krushna Kumari to relieve me of all my miseries and bring me happiness and prosperity." Krushna Kumari died in 1894, leaving behind a son and a daughter. His son's name was Moini Mohan Senapati.

He is aptly called the Thomas Hardy of Odisha (by Dr. Mayadhar Mansinha). Though he translated from Sanskrit, wrote poetry and attempted many forms of literature, he is now known primarily as the father of modern Odia prose fiction. The four novels of Fakir Mohan, written before 1897 and 1915 depicted the socio-cultural conditions of Odisha during the eighteenth and the nineteenth centuries. While the novels "Chha maana Atha Guntha", "Mamu" and "Prayaschita" explore the realities of social life in its multiple dimensions, "Lachhama" is a historical romance, dealing with the anarchical conditions of Odisha in the wake of Maratha invasions during the eighteenth century. **Chha**

Maana Atha Guntha is the first Indian novel dealing with how the landless peasants were exploited by the feudal lords. It was written much before the October revolution of Russia or much before the emerging of Marxist ideas in India. Fakir Mohan is also the writer of the first autobiography in Odia, "Atma Jeevan Charita."

His "Rebati" (1898) is widely given recognition as the first Odia short story. "Rebati" is the story of a young innocent girl whose intense desire for getting educated is presented in the context of a conservative society in a backward Odisha village which is hit by the killer epidemic cholera. His other stories are "Patent Medicine", "Daka Munshi", "Adharma Bitta", "Randi Pua Ananta" etc. "Randipua Ananta" is a widely acclaimed book written by him. He wrote a long poem *Ukkala Bhramanam* which first appeared in 1892. It means literally Tour of Odisha but actually is a commentary on the state of affairs in the Odisha at that time. It was written in a satirical manner.

Vyasa Kabi Fakir Mohan Senapati had a major role to play in the formation of Odisha and the acknowledgement of Odia language during the British period. He played a great role in establishing the distinct identity of Odisha, a languge spoken in the Indian State of Odisha. Fakir Mohan is distinguished as the father of Odia nationalism and modern Odia literature.

Chapter VIII

Kalindi Charan Panigrahi

Kalindi Charan Panigrahi (2 july 1901-15 May 1991) earned prominence as a noted Odia poet, novelist, story writer, dramatist and essayist. He was one of the members of the Odia literary group Sabuja Goshthi (the Green Group). He was influenced by the romantic thoughts of Tagore. Kalindi Charan Panigrahi, the elder brother of Bhagabati Charan Panigrahi, the founder of Marxist trend in Odisha, formed a group in 1920 called "Sabuja Samiti" together with two of his writer friends Annada Shankar Ray and Baikuntha Patnaik. Later on Kalindi Charan Panigrahi wrote his famous novel *Matira Manisha* influenced by Gandhism. He was for the time being the editor of English journals, *Bhanja Pradipa* and *Mayurbhanja Chronicle*. He had a great contribution for the independence of India though he was imprisoned illegally and tortured by the British. His eldest daughter Nandini Satpathy was born in 1931 who later went on to become the Chief Minister of Odisha. His great grandson Suparno Satpathy is a writer of repute, a social activist and a young political leader.

His major works are : poems like *Jadu Ghara, Puri Mandira* and *Mahadipa*. His novels include *Matira Manisha* (1934), *Luhara Manisha, Amarachita, Aajira Manisha* and *Mukta Godara Kshudha*. His short stories are : *Devadashi, Rashi Phala, Shesha Rashmi, Sagarika* and dramas are *Padmini* and *Pridarshi*. His biographical works are : *Bhakta*

Kabi Madhusudana, Karmabira Gauri Shankar, Jaba Ange Nibhaichi (autobiography) and essays like *Sahitya-Samachara* and *Sahityika*.

Kalindi Charan Panigrahi was given the honour of fellowship in Sahitya Academi in 1971. In the same year, he was awarded Padma Bhushan by Government of India. In 1976, Sambalpur University conferred on him honorary D.Lit Degree.

Chapter IX
Sitakanta Mahapatra

Sitakant Mahapatra is a noted Indian poet and a literary critic in Odia as well as English. He was in the Indian Administrative Service since 1961 until his retirement in 1995 and has since held exofficio posts such as the Chairman of National Book Trust, New Delhi. Apart from publishing 15 poetry collection, 5 essays collections, a writing about travel, over 30 contemplative works he had also translated many books. His poetry collection have been published in several Indian languages.

He was born in September 17, 1937 in village Mahanga situated on the banks of Chitrotpala, a tributary of the great Mahanadi. He started growing up reciting a chapter of Odia versian of Bhagwad Gita in a traditional household. After receiving his.cducation from Korua government high school, he joined Ravenshaw College, Cuttack (then affiliated with Utkal University). There he did his BA in History Honours in 1957 followed by Master's degree in Political Science from Allahabad University in 1959 where he started writing both in English and Odia, being the editor of the University journal. Later on he decided to write poetry wholly in his native language Odia as he had such realisation that that a poet could express his emotions fully and spontaneously in the language of his own. He had works also in English. In 1969, he did Development Studies at Cambridge University under Colombo Plan Fellowship. After that in 1988, he spent a year in Harvard

University participating in the Ford Foundation fellowship programme.

He taught for two years at Post Graduate Department of Utkal University before taking Indian Administrative Servies Examination. He joined the IAS in 1961 as the first Odia to top the statewide examination. He went on to hold many important posts like Secretary, Ministry of Culture, Government of India, and President, UNESCO's World Decade for Cultural Development (1994-1996). He was in many other high positions including those of senior : Fellow of Harvard University, Honorary Fellow of International Academy of Poets, Cambridge University etc.

His first collection of poetry in Odia, *Dipti O Dyuti* was published in 1963, his second anthelogy *Ashtapadi* in 1967, winning him the Odisha Sahitya Academy award. He had also published 350 poems in Odia and about 30 publications in English on literary criticism and culture. He studied tribals of Eastern India on a Homi Bhabha Fellowship (1975-1977) for two years. He has also two books on social anthropology published by the Oxford University Press. These books deal with the relationship between the old ritual based society and state sponsored development and explores the reason behind development programmes, failing in tribal areas despite state efforts. He established close relationship with the tribals and Santal tribal culture and the Santali language leading to the publication of nine anthologies of oral poetry of the tribals which he not only collected but also translated.

His notable works are : *Ashtapadi* 1963, *Shabdara akasha* 1971, *Aradrushya* 1981, *Shrestha Kavita* 1994, (all poetry), *Sabda, Svapna O nirvikata,* 1990 (essays), *Aneka Sarata* 1981 (travelogue), *Ushavilasa,* 1996 (palm leaf manuscript), in English : *The Ruined Temple and Others Poems,* 1996 (Poetry, translation) ; and *Unending Rhythms* (Oral poetry of Indian tribals in translation). He received many awards in cluding the Orissa Sahitya Academy Award,

1971 and 1984, for his poetry collection Sabdar Akash (the sky of the words) the Sahitya Academi Award, 1974, Sarala Award, 1985, culminating in India's highest literary honour the Jnanpith Award in 1993 for his contribution to Indian literature. In 2002, he was honoured by the Government of India with a Patma Bhushan. In 2011, he was awarded the Patma Vibhushan, the second highest civilian award of India, got also lifetime achievement award for literature at the 49th SAARC Literature festival at Agra. In fact though deeply touched within western literature, his pen has the rare touch of native soil.

Chapter X

Gopala Chandra Praharaj

Gopala Chandra Praharaj (September 9, 1874 - May 16, 1945) was a writer and linguist in the Odia language. He was also well-known as the compiler of the *Purnachandra Odia Bhashakosha*. He had great contributions to Odia literature by his prose-works. Though he was a lawyer by profession, he wrote several satirical and analytical essays, in magazines such as *Utkal Sahitya, Rasachakra, Nababharata, Satya Samachar,* regarding social, political and cultural issues of contemporary Odisha during early 20th century.

Praharaj was born on Sepetember 9, 1874 in an aristocratic zaminder Brahmin family of Siddheswarpur in the district of Cuttack. He completed his matriculation from Ravenshaw Collegeate School and studied FA from Ravenshaw College of Cuttack. He studied law at Calcutta University and became a lawyer in 1902.

He started writing essays in the Magazine Utkal Sahitya in 1901 by the caption "Bhagabata Tungire Sandhya", the first published work of the author. It was followed by "Bai Mohanty Panji" and many other writings on socio-cultural and political issues. He was the follower of Fakir Mohan Senapati and made a notable development in Odio satirical literature. Praharaj used the colloquial speech of Odisha and also Hindustani, Parsi, English, Sanskrit and folk languge in his prose works. He wrote several critical essays with different pen names in many magazines up to his old age. However he dedicated his life to the compilation of *Purnachandra Odia Bhashakosha*.

Purnachandra Odia Bhashakosha is the most remarkable lexicon (dictionary) in Odia language. It presents the meaning of words in four languages—Odia, English, Hindi and Bengali and clarifies the origin, development and the use of words. It contains 9,500 pages and 185 thousand words in 7 volumes. Praharaj not only compiled the lexicon but also raised funds for its publication and supervised its printing and sale. Praharaj included in this lexicon the words used in literature but also words of common speech. The publication of the lexicon had the patronage of the kings/princes of several princely states of the present Orissa. It is still regarded as the biggest dictionary in Oriya language, though few copies of the original printed version survive.

Praharaj was a great satirist of early 20th century. His essays some of which published in the shape of books mainly deal with social issues, political situations of Orissa and India and social-cultural mentality of contemporary people ; also the style of the essays was humorous and the essays were written in a critical manner. His remarkable writings are : — *Bhagabata Tungire Sandhya, Bai Mohanty Panji, Dunia ra Halchal, Nananka Bastani*. Some of his writings are difficult to obtain.

Praharaj's book *Utkalara Kohani* deals with the folk stories of Odisha. Among the remarkable works of Praharaj is "Dhaga Dhamali Rachana" containing the idioms of Odia language. His other works are his autobiography, many poems and stories for children, a book *i.e. Bhasa Kosha Safar*.

Chapter XI

Gopynath Mohanty

Gopinath Mohanty (1914-1991) was the winner of the prestigious Jnanpith award. He earned a great deal of eminence as Odia novelist of the mid-twentieth century and was the greatest Odia writer after Fakir Mohan Senapati. He and his older brother Kahnu Charan Mohanty, had a great influence on Odiya literature for three decades. He was born at Nagabali (a village on the bank of River Mahanadi), in Cuttack district on April 20, 1914. He was highly educated at Ravenshaw College and got his MA degree from Patna University in 1936. He joined the Odisha Administrative service in 1938. He spent most part of his service career among the poor tribals of the undivided Koraput District. He retired from government service in 1969. By the invitation of Professor Prabhat Nalini Das, founder, professor and Head of the English Department, Utkal University he was UGC distinguished visiting professor of the English Department, Utkal University in the late 1970s. In 1986, he joined San Jose State University in the USA as an Adjunct Professor of Social Sciences and died there on August 20, 1991.

He was the winner of the Central Sahitya Akademy Award in 1955 for his novel, *Amrutara Santana*. The Jnanpith Award was conferred on him in 1973 for his epicprose "Mati Matala" (The Fertile Soil). He won also the Soviet Land Nehru Award in 1970 for his Odia translation of Gorky's work, the D.Litt Degree by Sambalpur University in 1976 and a Fellowship for creative writing in Odia by the U.G.C. in 1979. In 1981, he was awarded Padma Bhushan by the Government of India for his significant contribution to literature.

Gopinath made his appearance on the literary scene at Post Independent Age. Both rural as well as tribal life of Odisha had their expression in the works of the writer. In the fiction, he took initiative to explore all aspects of Odishan life. He had a unique prose style of writing, choosing words and phrases from the speeches of ordinary men and women. Gopinath's first novel *Maha Gahirara Chasa* published in 1940, was followed by **Dadi Buddha** (1944), *Paraja* (1945) and *Amrutara Santaṇa* (1947). He had the publication of 24 novels, 10 collected short stories, added by three plays, two biographies, two volumes of critical essays, five books on the languges of Kandh, Gadaba and Saora tribes. Besides, he translated Tolstoy's *War and Peace (Yuddh O Shanti* in three volumes' 1985 - 86) and Tagore's *Jogajog* (translated in 1965) into Odia.

His novels like *Dadi Buddha, Paraja Amrutara Santana* and *Aphanca* are noteworthy because of their portrayal of tribal life. *Dadi Buddha,* a short novel of Gopinath Mohanty earned a great deal of distinction because of its being based on tribal life. The novel deals with the story of the decaying aspects of a tribal community under the influence of modern civilization. *Dadi Buddha* is an ancient date-palm standing for the cultural heritage of the tribal people as revealed in their age-old rituals and costumes. The tree is a silent witness representing the joys and sorrows of the tribal folk.

Paraja is a story of one's attachment to land, the soil of one's ancestors. In *Dadi Buddha*, the old order is replaced by the new, on the other hand, in *Paraja*, the element of brutality, creating hatred and violence. *Amrutara Santana,* the first Indian novel to receive Sahitya Akademi Award

(1955) centres round the life of Kandhas, another tribe in the southern part of Odisha. The novel reveals the grandeur of living and the intensity of suffering of the tribal people. Gopinath Mohanty has acknowledged his most important work being *Amrutara Santana.*

Gopinath's fictional world is not only confirmed to the tribal people. He has also written about the people of the coastal plains. Even when he changes his focus, from the hills to the plains, he has his deep concern for the oppressed and underprivileged as finding expression in his novel *Harijan* (1948). *Danapani* (1955) presents the world of petty, mean middle class ; full of gossips and rumours. *Laya Bilaya* (1961) is the exploration of the psyclological complexity of three members of a family from Kolkata to Puri. *Matimatala* (1964) being a novel of epic dimension, is based on life in rural Odisha and is the celebration of the eternity of love. He in this novel, makes a successful blending of the two worlds—the private world of lovers and the public world of social workers. Gopinath's language is significant for its poetic quality. Characters and landscapes became vivid and lifelike through different types of descriptions. His language is characterised for its unique quality and lyrical beauty.

In the post independence era Odia fiction took a new direction. The trend which Fakir Mohan Senapati has started actually developed more after 50's of last century. Gopinath Mohanti is one of the pioneers of a new trend, that of developing the individual as protagonest in Odia fiction. In his short stories Gopinath Mohanti highlights all aspects of Odishan life : life both in plains and the hills. In his stories also he discovers a unique prose style, choosing words and phrases from day to day speech of ordinary men and women.

Four of Gopinath's novels, *Paraja, Danapani*, *Laya Bilaya* and *Dadi Buddha,* have appeared in English translation. The first three have been translated by Bikram. K. Das and the last mentioned by one of Arun Kumar Mohanty. The English version of Paraja was published by Faber and Faber (UK) and Oxford University Press (India) in 1987. *The Survivor*, the English translation of *Danapani*, was published by Macmillon India Limited in 1995. The translation of Laya Bilaya bearing the title *High Tide, Ebb Tide* has been published by Lark books. *The Ancestor*, the translation of Gopinath's *Dadi Buddha*, has been brought out by the *Sahitya Akademi*. Besides a number of short stories of Gopinath have been translated. Translators have attempted to convey the richness and complexity of the original texts to readers unfamiliar with Odia.

In his portrayal of tribal life, Gopinath Mohanty stands in comparison with the Nigerian novelist Chinua Achebe. At one point, their visions are almost the same : they visualise the disintegration of a primitive community under the influence of a new faith. Gopinath highlights the unpleasant condition of colonialism in his work. Though Gopinath made experiments with various literary forms, he will be best remembered for his novels. He once said in an interview to Indian Literary Review, "Fiction, I realized would best suit my purpose." He takes novel to portray several dimensions of human existence. He draws materials of his writing from his rich experience and transforms it into a powerful image of life with his imagination.

Chapter XII
Sunanda Patnaik

Sunanda Potnaik was born in November 7, 1934, is an Indian classical singer of Gwalior gharana from Odisha. She was popularly known as "guruma". She is regarded as one of the great pioneers of Hindustani music. She is the daughter of legendary Oriya poet Baikunthanath Patnaik. She started singing at All India Radio in Cuttack in 1948 at the age of 14. Odisha Governor Asaf Ali having heard her once on radio, was very impressed with her singing and she became a regular singer at Raj Bhavan whenever the governor had guests. Once, President Rajendra Prasad heard her song at Puri. Quite impressed with her singing, he arranged her training under Pandit Vinayak Rao Pattavardhan at Pune with a scholarship. She was awarded with a degree of Masters in Music by Pune school in 1956. She had performances at All India Sadrang Sangeet Sammelan in Kolkata in September 1957 where she received 13 gold coins. After that, she performed at many concerts in India and is known on international level. She is well-known for her tarana which she sings at a high pace and is considered to be one of the best contemporary interpreters of Odissi music. She has been staying at Kolkata since 1983.

She was the receiver of Odisha Sangeet Natak Akademi award in 1970 and 1971. She received Indian lifetime achievement award in 2009 and lifetime achievement award from The Orissa Society of the America (OSA) in 2012. She also received Sangeet Natak Academy award (Tagore

Akadami Puraskar) for the year 2012. The degree of doctor of literature was conferred to her by the Utkal University in 1999 and the degree of doctor of music was conferred by the Akhil Bharatiya Gandharva Mahavidyalaya Mandal in 1975. *Nilamadhaba* is a National Film Award winning documentary film about her. The film was directed by Sri Dilip Patnaik and produced by Films Division. It was the winner of the "Best Biographical Documentary" for the year 2010 at the 58th National Film Awards in India.

Chapter XIII
Ramakanta Rath

Ramakanta Rath (Odia), was born in December 13, 1934 at Cuttack, Odisha, being one of the most well-known modern poets in the Odia literature. Being influenced by the poets like T.S. Eliot and Ezra Pound, Rath made great experiments with form and style. A search for anything that is mystic, the riddles of life and death, loneliness of individual selves, to attain mundane needs and desires are the main themes of this philosopher cum poet. His poetry touches on a sense of pessimism together with a sense of beauty but he was not mentally prepared to disguise himself under the guise of a preacher of goodness and absolute beauty. His poetry has the touch of melancholy and also a touch of lamentation on the inevitability of death and the feeling of futility. The poetic touches as revealed in his creations express a remarkable sign of symbolic awareness to spritual contents of life. Often he transcends beyond ordinary human capabilities to reach the higher territories of sharp intellectualism. His subject matter varies from the modern interpretation of ancient Sanskrit literature *i.e.* protagonist Radha in the poem "Sri Radha" to the everpresent death consciousness, as revealed in "Saptama Ritu" (The Seventh Season).

Regarding his educational qualifications he attained his degree on MA in English literature from Ravenshaw College in Odisha. Though he joined the Indian Administrative service in 1957, he went on continuing his writing career.

He had his retirement as Chief Secretary Odisha after working in several important posts in the Central Government such as Secretary to the Government of India. He was awarded the Sahitya Akadami Award in 1977, Saraswathi Samman in 1992, Bishuva Samman in 1990 and the Padma Bhushan in 2006, Indians third highest civilian honour. He was the Vice-president of the Sahitya Academy of India from 1993 to 1998 and the President of the Sahitya Akademi of India from 1998 to 2003, New Delhi. In February 2009, he was given a fellowship by the Cental Sahitya Akademi, the fifth Odia writer to be given such honour.

His major works are poems : • *"Kate Dinara"* (Of a Long Long Time) 1962.

• "Aneka Kothari" (Many Rooms), 1967. • "Sandigdha Mrigaya" (Suspicious Hunting), 1971. • "Saptama Ritu" (The Seventh Season), 1977. • "Sachitra Andhara" (Picturesque Darkness), 1982.

Long Poems :

• "Sri Radha" (Sri Radha), 1984, (making him win Saraswati Samman in 1992, for this poetry), • "Sri Palataka" (Mr-Escapist), 1997.